WRITING

UNDE[R]

Teac[hin]g writing in the Primary School

Edited by

Judith Graham and Alison Kelly

CLEAR

**The Centre for Language Education
and Research**

This book has been written by the Language/English Teaching
Studies Team at Roehampton Institute London

Contributions from: Rebecca Bunting, Fiona M. Collins,
Judith Graham, Alison Kelly, Liz Laycock, Pat Pinsent, Anne Washtell

David Fulton Publishers

London

Published in association with Roehampton Institute, London

David Fulton Publishers Ltd
Ormond House, 26–27 Boswell Street, London WC1N 3JD

First published in Great Britain by David Fulton Publishers 1998

Note: The right of Judith Graham and Alison Kelly to be identified as the editors of this work has been asserted by them in accordance with the Copyright, Designs and Patents Act 1988.

British Library Cataloguing in Publication Data
A catalogue record for this book is available from the British Library

ISBN 1–85346–554–2

Typeset by Textype Typesetters, Cambridge
Printed in Great Britain by The Cromwell Press Ltd, Trowbridge, Wilts.

Contents

Preface

As we approach the end of the century and the millennium, literacy, and the school's role in teaching literacy, is enjoying the highest profile. All but a handful of schools in the country are instituting a daily 'literacy hour' in which the explicit teaching of reading and writing takes place. In our book, *Reading Under Control*, we examined the teaching of reading, its history, its methods, its routines, resources and recurring issues. This companion volume does the same for writing which, as a process, develops alongside reading, provided that both are taught and supported as rewarding, meaningful and purposeful activities. Many physical, cognitive and affective demands are made on children as they develop as writers and we inspect all the various elements in this book. Teachers and student teachers should be strengthened in their understanding of how writing can be taught and valued, and they should be enabled to create a breadth and variety of writing experiences in which children can learn competence, confidence and enjoyment.

The contributors have been able to include accounts of teachers and children at work thanks to examples supplied by their students, their colleagues, and classroom teachers with whom they have worked. In particular they would like to thank Sarah Arscott, Jan Avery, Angela Buckle, Karin Doull, Gaye Grundy, Ruth Hunter, Gail Kelly, Fiona Kemp, Alexandra Law, Jeune Persaud, Heidi McCluskey, Susie Midgeley, Sue Robson, Sue Smedley, Alison Townsend, Geraldine Woods and the teachers at Horn Park and Cardwell Schools, Greenwich.

We apologise for not attributing the dictation passage which occurs on page vii. We have been unable to locate its source.

We are most grateful to Dr Anita Jackson and Dr Gillian Lathey, Roehampton Institute, London.

And thanks also to Conrad Guettler and Mark Pawley for patient support and unflagging interest.

Judith Graham and Alison Kelly
Roehampton Institute
July 1998

Contributors

Rebecca Bunting is Assistant Dean and coordinates the MA in English, Language and Literacy. She was inner-London coordinator for the LNC Project and her research interests are in the areas of literacy and linguistics in an educational context. She is the author of *Teaching About Language in the Primary School* (Fulton).

Fiona M. Collins is Senior Lecturer and coordinator of the Language Teaching Studies. Her research interests are in children's literature, popular culture and visual literacy. She was involved in the *Gathering of Evidence of Children's Reading* video for SCAA and contributed to Roehampton's Survey of Children's Reading to be published as *Young Children's Reading at the End of the Century*.

Judith Graham is Principal Lecturer with interests and teaching commitments in all areas of literacy and children's literature. Her previous teaching has been in inner-London schools, at the Institute of Education and at the University of Greenwich, once Avery Hill College. She is the author of *Pictures on the Page* (NATE), *Cracking Good Books* (NATE) and co-editor (with Alison Kelly) of *Reading Under Control* (Fulton).

Alison Kelly is Senior Lecturer in Language Education. She worked for many years as a primary teacher in London as a class teacher, a peripatetic teacher for Traveller families and an advisory teacher for Language. She teaches on undergraduate, postgraduate and INSET courses and has interests in all aspects of children's literacy learning. She co-edited with Judith Graham *Reading Under Control* (Fulton).

Liz Laycock is Principal Lecturer in Education and was coordinator of Language Teaching Studies for six years. She is Programme Convener of the Primary PGCE Programme with particular interests in early literacy, narrative, the teaching of children with English as an additional language, and the assessment of language and literacy.

Pat Pinsent has been for many years Principal Lecturer in English and is currently concerned in the Distance Learning mode of the MA in Children's Literature. Current research interests include children's literature, reading development, poetry, and equality issues, especially as reflected in information books. She edited *The Power of the Page* and wrote *Children's Literature and the Politics of Equality* (both Fulton).

Anne Washtell is Senior Lecturer contributing to all language and literacy courses. She is particularly interested in early literacy development, the development of phonemic awareness in children and supporting children with reading difficulties.

Introduction

A teacher dictates this passage to his class of 80 nine year olds:

> While hewing yews, Hugh lost his ewe
> And put it in the hue and cry.
> You brought the ewe back by and by
> And only begged the hewer's ewer,
> Your hands to wash in water pure.

The children write carefully in their copybooks using copperplate handwriting. Older children – monitors – walk up and down the rows to check that the children are working hard and sitting up straight.

This is what a writing lesson might have looked like one hundred years ago when learning to write consisted of imitating adult models – copying or tracing letters, memorising spellings, and transcribing passages from the Bible, Latin grammar or, for light relief, Aesop's fables. Younger children would write on slates so their efforts were no sooner accomplished than they had to be rubbed out in readiness for the next exercise. The nearest the children got to their own compositions is described by Sybil Marshall:

> The teacher showed the children an object of some sort, and from the entire class, ranged in their rows of desks before her, she elicited 'facts' about the object which could then be written down, e.g. 'We have a plum. The plum is red. It has a stone. The plum grew on a tree.' The sentences, composed by the teacher from the children's hesitant observations, were then written by her on the blackboard, from where the children copied them in whatever form of script they had been taught to write.
> (1974, p. 2)

Now, take a leap forward one hundred years. A Reception class has been visited by a storyteller. One of her stories is a Native American creation tale about how the sun came into existence. Later, Matthew (age 5) dictates a story of his own to his teacher which she writes down for him:

> Once upon a time there was no such thing as a dog. There were just dogfish alive, until one day a dogfish came out of the sea and it started to live on land. While he was living on land some very peculiar things happened. He started to change. Instead of scales, it was fur. Instead of no neck, it had one. Instead of flippers, it had a tail. Instead of fins, it had legs. Until one day he was a dog! This way life on earth has developed ever since.

Despite the role reversal, both the Victorian teacher dictating and the contemporary teacher taking dictation could be described as being 'in control' of the teaching of writing. Both based their practice on prevailing views of the writing process, of the nature of learning and of the relationship between child and adult. The Victorian teacher would have believed that 'We must not expect young people to invent matter, what they write should be infused into them' (John Walker, 1801, in a book for teachers, cited in Michael, 1987; p. 313), and his concern would have been to give children adult models to imitate with an emphasis on correct spelling, handwriting and grammar. The contemporary teacher is just as concerned that her children use these aspects correctly, but knows too that composing is important and is giving her young writer the opportunity to compose with greater fluency than he would achieve if left to transcribe by himself. Early behaviourist thinking lies behind the often punitive Victorian regimes, where wrong spellings or poor handwriting could lead to the ultimate negative reinforcer – the cane. The contemporary teacher's interaction with a younger child suggests a more collaborative enterprise, where her adult model of expertise is still privileged but where it is exercised in a way that empowers the younger writer. The point is that we know much more now about the writing process and about the learner, and we bring this to bear on our teaching. Chapters 1 and 2 of this book chart the developing understanding about writing which has moulded the ways we teach writing.

We write this at a time of further change and challenge as the *National Literacy Strategy* (hereafter referred to as *NLS*) is being introduced (DfEE, 1998b). The framework it offers takes the National Curriculum for English as its starting point and goes on to prescribe exactly what we should teach and when; never before has the teaching of writing (and reading) been so externally controlled. The framework offers a teaching structure within its Text, Sentence and Word level work (see Chapter 3). There are many rich and imaginative suggestions for work and you will find that we make close links with these and the framework throughout the book. However, there are points to be made here about such tight external control – one potential hazard is that it may actually be disempowering for teachers as it can take away the need to rationalise and stand back from practice. An imposed framework tells us what we 'should' be doing, which is always superficially attractive but, in the process, it takes away the need for analytic thinking about what we practise. The changes that Pat Pinsent and Rebecca Bunting describe in their chapters came about partly because of the critical inspections teachers gave their own work in the light of new research. We would not want to lose sight of the role teachers and researchers have always had in shaping and understanding good literacy practice.

In *Reading Under Control* (1997) we said that 'control in any area springs from a secure understanding of processes and enabling practices'; it is this belief that motivates the structure and content of *Writing Under Control* and we suggest that such a feeling of control is more important than ever today. After the historical update provided by Chapters 1 and 2, we move firmly into the late twentieth century classroom with an account of the many different writing routines that are needed for the effective teaching of writing. In this chapter, Anne Washtell links these routines with the *NLS* framework and includes discussion of the resources teachers need as well. She also makes important points about the role of parents in children's writing lives. The next two chapters tackle the two distinct aspects of the writing process: composition and transcription. In Chapter 4, Fiona Collins looks at the demands of narrative, non-narrative and poetry writing and describes ways of supporting and scaffolding children's understanding of the complexities of composition. In Chapter 5, Alison Kelly looks in detail at the three separate aspects of transcription: spelling, punctuation and handwriting. Liz Laycock's chapter shows how crucial close observation, analysis and assessment are in shaping teaching and monitoring progress. She adds an informative section on SATs. Finally, Judith Graham's chapter draws the threads of the book together through its analysis of differences in the writing from children with literacy difficulties, boys and girls, and children with English as an Additional Language.

This book offers another framework then, one which is clearly linked with the *National Curriculum* and the *NLS*, but which is intended to offer you, the teacher or prospective teacher, a sense of control in all aspects of the teaching of writing. This sense of control is one which is achieved through clear understanding of all of the above; it is about knowing where we have come from in the teaching of writing and of how current views have shaped and changed practice. It should also arm you in readiness for any new initiatives that may be on their way!

There is another kind of knowledge that is important too; personal control also comes about when we feel confident about the subject we are teaching. An important strand of this book deals with the subject knowledge teachers need, at their own level, to inform their planning and assessment. Those of you who are in initial teacher education are required to meet the requirements of *Circular Number 4/98* (DfEE, 1998a) which is the National Curriculum for teacher education. As well as requirements which relate to what is needed for teaching, there is also a section on 'Trainees' Knowledge and Understanding of English' which is intended to ensure that you have a confident grasp of language and how it works. You will find that *Writing Under Control* addresses this area in the following places:

Ciricular Number 4/98 (pp. 24–6)	*Writing Under Control*
a **the nature and role of standard English**	Chapters 2 ,6, 7
b **the spoken and written language**	
systems of English	
LEXICAL	
Graphology	Chapters 5 (Spelling, Handwriting), 6, 7
How the writing system	
addresses the sound system	Chapter 5 (Spelling), 6, 7
Morphology	Chapter 5 (Spelling)
Word meanings	Chapters 4, 5 (Spelling)
GRAMMATICAL	
Grammar	Chapters 2, 4, 5, 6, 7
Punctuation	Chapter 5, 6, 7
TEXTUAL	
Cohesion	Chapter 4
Layout	Chapter 4
Organisation	Chapters 2, 4, 6
c **evaluating texts**	Chapter 4
d **technical terms:**	
Sub-lexical	Glossaries in Chapter 5
Textual	Chapters 2, 4

This Circular gives abundant detail on the main interdependent components involved in writing. It gives less attention to more global considerations, though it states clearly that trainee teachers 'need to know how to teach writing so that pupils write confidently, accurately, fluently and with understanding' (p. 19). In our work with student teachers, we often gather writing histories from them in which our students attribute their writing confidence and competence as writers to such experiences as: a teacher becoming excited or informed by a piece of their writing; a teacher setting up a dialogue in writing with them enabling the work to be extended over a long period ('interactive writing'); the incentive of a diary or attractive notebook for private writing; the realisation that writing can, on some occasions, meet a creative need such as might equally be met by making a painting or a piece of music; the excitement of seeing ideas come forth as you write; the understanding that writing can, at difficult times, serve as a solace and an outlet for strong feelings; and the satisfaction of seeing a piece through to a perfect end product. These personal revelations about the role and power of writing are very relevant to your appreciation of the writing process and should frame and inform the reading of this book.

For children to be in control of writing a confident grasp of all aspects of the writing process is needed and this is why we are so insistent that an important strand of teaching writing is developing a healthy curiosity about language. Such curiosity should be fostered both with regard to the shapes and features of texts (narrative, non-narrative etc., Chapter 4), and with regard to the transcriptional aspect of writing (spelling, punctuation and handwriting, Chapter 5). We want children to delight in the curiosities and challenges of our spelling and punctuation systems rather than be fearful or inhibited by them. A prevailing theme of the book is ensuring that our teaching leaves children clearly free to attend to particular aspects of the writing, whether this is attention needed for developing the structure of a story, character delineation, sentence construction or appropriate punctuation.

As in *Reading Under Control,* our preoccupation is with good teaching and with doing the very best possible work with children. Learning to write is an extraordinary feat and, as children become writers, we get glimpses of them at their most active, creative and imaginative. Children can surprise and delight us, as they learn that writing enables them to 'create worlds' (Smith, 1984; p. 152). The Dogfish story (p. 1) contains many different influences, ranging from the traditional story Matthew had heard in school to the final line which he told his teacher he had heard on a video soundtrack. Yet its freshness both startles and engages the reader. When children discover that they can create such 'secondary worlds' then it is their turn to feel in control and empowered.

CHAPTER 1

From Copying to Creation: the teaching of Writing before the 1980s

Pat Pinsent

TEACHING WRITING BEFORE 1960

Let us look at the experience of an imaginary English teacher – Mary Angell – who was born in the 1930s. Her early schooling, broken up by the Second World War, included such things as making many copies of 'headlines' in a copperplate hand. The intention of this (which seldom succeeded) was to inculcate handwriting skills, but the process also provided unwanted and decontextualised information, such as 'Linseed oil is derived from flax'. The whole process certainly conveyed the lesson that copying from adult models was the way to learn. This was supported by copying passages from books chosen by the teacher, and reproducing from memory stories read to the class. Twenty years earlier there had been isolated, more imaginative initiatives such as that quoted by Shayer (1972) of a teacher who said, 'The best way, indeed the only way, to learn to write is to try to write'. He went on to provide interesting assignments like describing a sea-monster (p. 81) but if Mary's teachers had heard about these they gave no indication of this in their lessons.

At grammar school, Mary's English education was extended by grammatical exercises and the requirement to write compositions about abstract topics such as 'Patriotism' or letters to non-existent recipients about holidays which did not take place. Comprehension, précis, and accurate renditions of literary texts selected for examination rounded off the English curriculum. Mary therefore internalised the message that correct set pieces were what mattered.

When she went to college in September 1953, to be trained as a teacher on a two year course, Mary received conflicting messages. It was difficult to reconcile the narrow approach of 'Methods' (practical teaching approaches) courses with the kind of 'child-centred' approach which was beginning to appear in Educational Studies (educational theory). One of her assessed essays had been based on a quotation from Robert Browning:

> . . . To know
> rather consists in opening out a way
> whence the imprisoned splendour may escape,
> than in effecting entry for a light
> supposed to be without . . .
> (Paracelsus, 1835; I)

You may recognise this as a poetic 'empty vessels' type of argument!

Mary started work in a secondary modern school with many naive hopes about her career but little firm grasp of how to teach her subject, as what she had learnt at college tended to replicate the way she had been taught herself. The kind of English teaching expected from her gave little credence to her pupils' bringing with them to school any kind of inner light, or even any kind of knowledge about life or the writing process. The sole audience for writing in school was the teacher, and so little were the results valued that exercise books, once full, landed in the wastepaper basket. Mary felt that if she had been teaching younger children, there might have been more opportunity to liberate her pupils' 'imprisoned splendour'. In fact, there were very similar pressures in primary school (with the eleven-plus examination) and no greater understanding of children's development as writers.

CREATIVE WRITING

In 1963, Mary, now Mrs Bright, returned to teaching after six years of bringing up her own children. She found herself readily welcomed, despite her secondary background, in the local primary school. Confessing herself out of touch, even in her own subject, she was heartened to read Sybil Marshall's *Experiment in Education* (1963) which had just been published. Marshall describes teaching in a village school during and after the Second World War. She discovered, while teaching in a cross-curricular way which combined music, art and writing, that the quality of the children's work in all these areas was greatly improved. Mary recognised how the ideals of educational theory which she had found exciting in her Educational Studies initial training, and which had been fortified by her experience with her own young children, could be brought to life in the classroom.

At this period, 'creative writing', under various names, was in full swing in primary schools. Over the next few years Mary read and implemented with enthusiasm the recommendations of Margaret Langdon (1961), Boris Ford (1963), Sheila Lane and Marion Kemp (1967) and many others. The title of Alec Clegg's book, *The Excitement of Writing* (1964), conveyed the enthusiasm these writers brought to their subject, and, as in the other books, it also included a collection of children's own work, showing the immense potential of child writers. David Holbrook's *English for the Rejected* (1964) gave an account of amazing results achieved with young people who had been written off by society. All the books abounded in ideas of how to foster similar qualities in other young writers. Basil Maybury's *Creative Writing for Juniors* (1967) advocated working through sense stimuli of touch, sight and taste to encourage writing. He suggested using, for instance, music as a stimulus, blowing bubbles or, more daringly, setting fire to paper.

Behind much of this creative writing was more general theory. Sybil Marshall, who later became Reader in Education at Sussex University, acknowledges in *Creative Writing* (1974) being influenced by Suzanne Langer, on whose work Marshall's definition of creative writing is based. She says creativity is 'the ability to create one's own symbols of experience: creative writing is the use of written language to conceptualise, explore and record experience in such a way as to create a unique symbolisation of it.' (p. 10).

Mary sometimes found it difficult to avoid the creative writing lesson falling into a limited pattern like, 'Listen to this music . . . what does it make you feel . . . now write a story . . .' Nor did she feel comfortable criticising writing which clearly came out of the children's feelings. Sometimes the results were not very interesting and she wondered if she really was using the best way of drawing out the children's own experience, let alone building on it. It was difficult for someone not trained in psychoanalysis to be alert to the 'symbolic meaning', to how 'children's creative work symbolises . . . the quest for integration of the identity. . . ' (Holbrook, 1967; p. 3). She knew too that she should not neglect the tools of the trade like spelling and handwriting and had to admit that her pupils' strengths in writing stories and poems might not always help them much in the more subject based curriculum of the secondary school, nor, indeed, with the practical written demands of life.

LANGUAGE AND LEARNING

It was partly because of feelings of inadequacy in this area, and partly to increase her professional standing, that Mary took advantage of the Open University's scheme to award credit rating for previous study, thus facilitating non-graduate teachers obtaining a degree. Teachers were particularly encouraged to select courses relevant to their professional interests, so Mary chose 'Language and Learning'. The course reader was entitled *Language in Education* (Cashdan and Grugeon, 1972) and among the papers included in it were several particularly relevant to the teaching of English. Mary read with interest James Britton's 'What's the use? A schematic account of language functions'. This article had a practical aim in mind, the classifying of 2000 pieces of writing from pupils aged 11 to 18, and it also was convincingly grounded in the earlier theoretical studies of Harding (1937), Langer (1951) and Moffett (1968). Although Britton's classroom based research was initially concerned with secondary school pupils, it was not long before its results filtered into primary schools by way of the Bullock Report, *A Language for Life* (1975).

The Bullock Report, which appeared in the concluding year of Mary's degree studies, became sacred scripture to Mary and her colleagues. The language functions identified by Britton and his team in 1972 were described thus in Bullock:

> The three main categories . . . are Transactional, Expressive and Poetic. The Expressive is the central one. It is language 'close to the speaker', often the language used by intimates in a shared context . . . it provides the tentative stage through which a pupil's new thinking must pass on its way to the comparative certainty of knowledge.
> (p. 165).

The Transactional mode is defined as using language with the intention of getting things done, as in advertisements or regulations, while the Poetic mode, not confined to poetry only, stands back from the subject described. Elsewhere in the Bullock Report, attention is given to the kind of audience for which children are writing (themselves, the teacher or the wider world). The recommendation is also made that pupils should have the opportunity to draft their work before submitting the finished article (pp. 166–7).

Mary began to incorporate a variety of different forms of writing that were not simply based on the expressive and sometimes poetic functions which she had up to now generally been demanding from her pupils. Rules about how to behave in school, advertisements for imaginary or even real products, accounts of events the children had experienced, all began to vie with story as outcomes of the English lesson. Her other lessons changed too. Instead of insisting that her top primary pupils write up scientific work in dictated formulae, she let them use an expressive mode to note for themselves what they had actually observed. She created opportunities for her children to write for real audiences. Like other teachers throughout the country, she encouraged her pupils to write to children in other schools, to local newspapers, to suppliers of educational material, as well as recognising the fact that they might well write for themselves alone, in personal journals which she promised she would not even attempt to look at unless invited.

Mary soon discovered that Britton's work was probably the best known out of a body of writing emanating from a number of educationalists influential in both initial and in-service teacher education. An account of the genesis of this movement was to be found in John Dixon's *Growth Through English*, first published in 1967 and reprinted many times. Based on a conference held for teachers of English in America and UK at Dartmouth, New England, in 1966, it presents the various paradigms of English teaching, the 'skills' model and the 'cultural heritage' model, before expressing its own endorsement of the 'personal growth' model, in which writing should express something that the writer feels is worth saying:

> Language is learnt in operation, not by dummy runs. In English, pupils meet to share their encounters with life . . . in ordering and composing situations that in some way symbolise life as we know it, we bring order and composure to our inner selves.
> (p. 13)

Mary and her colleagues were aware that some theorists such as Frank Whitehead (1978) did not welcome the approach of Britton and others to writing, but had she been asked her opinion she would have argued that the different functions had been very useful in extending the kinds of writing of her pupils, and their consciousness that they are writing for someone.

BEGINNING WRITING

Soon after completing her Open University degree in 1975, Mary found herself for the first time teaching a Reception class. At the same time, her taste for study had led her to start work on a Master's degree, so it seemed a natural development to look into the writing of these very young children. As someone initially trained for secondary teaching, she had always dreaded having, as she saw it, to impart so much basic knowledge to children who had not even made a start on literacy, so it came as something of a surprise to learn from the researchers, and from her own observations, that children in fact brought much more knowledge about writing into school than she had ever given them credit for. Margaret Clark's influential study of 32 children who were literate before going to school, *Young Fluent Readers* (1976), while focussed predominantly on their reading abilities, showed that many of these children were interested in writing even before they were four.

Mary was particularly fascinated by Marie Clay's *What Did I Write: Beginning Writing Behaviour* (1975), which charts the way in which children's earliest marks can be seen as representing discoveries of 'real' writing. These discoveries are only possible when the child sees people writing. Clay says:

The linear scribble that fills the lines of a writing pad has, for the child, all the mystery of an unfamiliar code. It stands for a myriad of possible things but does not convey a particular message. The child seems to say 'I hope I've said something important. You must be able to understand what I've said. What did I write?'
(p. 48)

Interpreting the 'linear scribble' of the five year olds in her class was both challenging and satisfying, but she wished she had known more about children's abilities when her own children had been young.

Mary also began to value the children's inventive attempts at spelling, and she learnt that as early as 1971, the research of Charles Read had explained how children use their awareness of the sounds of letters to enable them to write words without being explicitly taught by a teacher or parent. Carol Chomsky's 'Write now, read later' (1971), with its message that children could learn to read by creating their own spellings, was also congenial, particularly because it chimed in with her own discovery that young children could be helped towards reading by means of their own writing. An approach which recognised this was the 'Language Experience' approach which was published as *Breakthrough to Literacy* (McKay *et al.*, 1970). This material comprised plastic 'Sentence Makers' and little word cards which children could use to make their own line of writing, based on their own experience and what they said about it. Then they could transcribe it onto paper and draw a picture to go with it. She had seen it in use in other primary classrooms, but had some reservations about the repetitious sentence structures that emerged and the need to put all the little pieces back in the right places in their individual folders.

Mary's research and work with Reception class children had shown her that teaching writing and reading did not mean introducing them to something totally unfamiliar, but was a matter of helping them to build on what they already knew. She wanted her own small-scale research project to examine the nature of children's prior knowledge, so the kind of longitudinal study that Glenda Bissex had made of her own son in *GNYS AT WRK: a child learns to write and read* (1980) attracted her as a dissertation topic. The most important thing she had learned was never to underestimate young children.

Another revelation was the work of the Russian cognitive psychologist, Vygotsky, whose writings had been translated and published from 1962 onwards. On the subject of writing, Vygotsky was both provoking and illuminating. His account of the difficulties which young children face in learning to write made the process of teaching them seem almost impossible. The high level of abstraction required in order to 'replace words by images of words', to address 'an absent or imaginary person' without any real motivation, and to be aware of the necessary alphabetical symbols to put all this down on paper (1962, pp. 98–9), sounded as if it was well beyond her pupils, and certainly gave her an understanding of why some of them found learning to write problematic. Yet elsewhere Vygotsky's explanation of the 'zone of proximal development' gave her more encouragement as it showed how children might in fact learn this difficult process. He says, 'What a child can do with assistance today she will be able to do by herself tomorrow' (1978, p. 87). Mary realised that she had often found herself assisting pupils with the beginnings of writing and noticed that they were on the verge of achieving independence but needed just that little extra guidance towards it. The 'zone of proximal development defines those functions that have not yet matured but are in the process of maturation' (1978, p. 86).

CHILDREN'S WRITING DEVELOPMENT

Having worked with the youngest and the oldest pupils in the primary school, Mary Bright was naturally interested in the ways in which children's writing developed, and what might be expected from them at different ages. She found the Crediton research project (1980), directed by Andrew Wilkinson, gave her some information. The team had investigated the writing abilities of children aged seven, ten and thirteen, using a framework for analysis based on stages of cognitive, affective, moral, and stylistic development abstracted from the theoretical work of Moffett (1968) and Britton (1982). While the categories Wilkinson provides were far too complex for daily use in the classroom, Mary found that looking at a few pieces of children's writing in detail was quite illuminating. She felt that any research which makes the teacher more aware of some of the factors entering into child writers' perceptions about what they are doing, what they want to do, and who they are writing for, provides a useful tool for the teacher. Wilkinson and his colleagues remark that the work of Britton has the limitation of perhaps over-stressing the cognitive aspect, and ignoring the many others which enter into the child's writing development. Wilkinson also reminds us that 'We need to make assessments of children's development in order to help them develop further. In other words, assessment is to be regarded rather as a teaching than as a measuring device' (pp. 223–4).

As Mary handed in her dissertation in 1980, she pondered many things. How she taught English now was a world away from the copying and conformity to adult models that had been part of her childhood. She knew much more of approaches which put the child at the heart of the process; she knew the pros and cons of creative writing; she found understanding of functions, forms, and audiences enriched the range and quality of writing in her classroom; she looked at her very youngest children's writing with new eyes and understood her supportive role more clearly; she knew how valuable it was to analyse closely individual pupil's writing.

She reflected too that she had learnt most about the teaching of writing by engaging in her own writing. Many theorists she had read seemed to pay relatively little attention to the writing process as experienced by adults. Perhaps that was something for the future.

FURTHER READING

Allen, D. (1980) *English Teaching since 1965. How Much Growth?* London: Heinemann.
Marshall, S. (1963) *An Experiment in Education.* Cambridge: Cambridge University Press.

CHAPTER 2

From Process to Genre: recent developments in the teaching of Writing

Rebecca Bunting

This chapter discusses approaches to the teaching of writing in primary schools from the early 1980s to the late 1990s. It provides an overview of significant developments which will necessarily be rather selective and general, since a detailed historical survey of the period, with an account of why certain approaches and trends prevailed, would be the subject of an entire book.

The last twenty years in the history of the teaching of writing have been characterised by a growing understanding about writing on the part of teachers and researchers, particularly in relation to the nature of the process of writing and the nature of writing itself. This has included developments in the use of information and communications technology for writing. This period has also been characterised by controversy both about methodologies for teaching writing and about the very purposes of writing in school.

UNDERSTANDING THE PROCESS OF WRITING

Process writing

Recent approaches to writing emphasise the process of the writing rather than the end product. In a process approach, or process writing as it is also known, teachers recognise that much more attention must be paid to the development of a piece of writing, as writing is more than the simple eliciting of a product by the teacher; it is a process that involves thinking and shaping meaning. There are various stages to be gone through in the production of the final piece of writing and writers need support with these stages. A process approach views children as authors and treats their written work as creative and meaningful. Children's difficulties are treated as normal writers' difficulties, rather than failures of ability: so, for example, errors and misunderstandings need to be worked on, as a professional writer would, rather than punished by the teacher's red pen. A process approach encourages children to take more responsibility for their own writing, including decisions about revisions, corrections and presentation. Graves (1981) uses a property image in arguing for this approach: he says that 'owners' of their work are far more likely to take care of their 'property' than those who 'rent' their work from the teacher, to whom it really belongs. This image conveys the importance of children's interest and engagement with the writing process.

The distinction between the composition involved in writing and the transcriptional aspects of writing such as spelling, punctuation and handwriting is important in a process approach. Smith (1982) relates the composition aspect to the role of the author, and the transcription aspect to that of the secretary, a useful distinction for the developing writer. Fluent writers can attend to both these aspects concurrently, though with different degrees of attention, whereas young writers, Smith argues, need to attend to composition first and transcription later. Both are necessary and important but teachers should not try to develop the transcriptional skills at the expense of encouraging thinking and composing skills. This philosophy is in complete contrast to an approach which requires children to labour at spelling and punctuation exercises before being allowed to do some real writing.

A process approach often involves children reflecting on their own writing. This reflection could be on the written product, such as commenting on why certain decisions were made about what to include in the writing, or on the actual process of writing, such as how an effort was consciously made to vary sentence length. Often such reflection is achieved through the use of writing journals or writing partners, where children conduct dialogues with the teacher or their partner about their writing (see Chapter 3).

A process approach also involves strategic and supportive intervention by the teacher during the process of the writing, rather than the teacher sitting in judgement when it is all finished. Smith (1982), rather ghoulishly but appropriately, described this traditional marking of an end product as 'manicuring the corpse', trying to do something to improve the situation when it is too late. In this traditional model, children see writing as largely for assessment by the teacher, and they have only one attempt at the writing before handing it in, in what Richmond (1990) described as 'a fairground shooting game where you only have one shot'. These lessons about writing remain with us even much later in our lives, as Smith comments: 'Sitting on the shoulder of many writers is the wraith of a school teacher, waiting to jump on every fault of punctuation or spelling, on every infelicity of expression.' (Smith, 1982; p. 13).

One book in particular caught teachers' imaginations about the possibility of opening up the classroom as an environment to support writing development through a process approach. In *Writing: Teachers and Children at Work* (1983), Donald Graves advocates a workshop approach which focusses on the needs of the writer and uses the 'real' writer as a model. Graves carried out a longitudinal study of children learning to write in New Hampshire, USA and his findings led him to advocate a model of writing which incorporates pre-writing activities (such as brainstorming ideas), drafting, editing, proofreading and publishing. In this model, children are permitted to choose their own topics for writing, helped to revise their work for publication and, most importantly, encouraged to reflect on their own development as writers, sharing and collaborating on their work with their peers and their teacher (Graves calls this 'conferencing').

Graves also argues that teachers should themselves write with and for their children because teachers cannot teach writing without understanding the processes the young writer is going through and without being able to demonstrate aspects of writing to the learner: 'We don't find many teachers of oil painting, piano, ceramics or drama who are not practitioners in their field' (1983, p. 6).

Graves' influential model for teaching writing clearly complements Smith's promotion of the distinctions between composition and transcription in teaching writing. Together, they set an agenda which began to shape the teaching of writing in the 1980s and 1990s in the USA and beyond.

As the process approach gained momentum, so the centrality of the key concepts of audience and purpose for children's writing emerged. These concepts are not new concerns: even in 1975, the Bullock Report (see Chapter 1) was arguing that children should be writing for audiences other than the teacher, because 'if a child knows that what he [sic] is writing is going to interest and entertain others, he will be more careful with its presentation' (p. 166). However, greater accuracy was the spur behind the Bullock concept of audience; more recently, a sense of audience is seen as central to writing development because it gives children experience of writing different kinds of texts and of handling the complex relationship in their writing between writer and reader. This means that a writer has to make decisions about levels of formality and has to consider how explicit to be in the writing and what the audience already knows. These are key skills in becoming a writer but it is only relatively recently that they have been seriously considered in the classroom.

Writers need a sense of audience because the audience influences the tone, nature and form of the writing. Writers also need to understand the purpose of their writing and that writing differs according to both audience and purpose. Without this understanding, children are writing in an abyss, with no sense of why they are writing, what their intentions are in writing, and for whom they are writing. It follows that they need experience of writing for a range of audiences and a range of purposes and that opportunities for these must be made in the classroom. When the purpose for writing extends beyond practising skills, the writing curriculum becomes reinvigorated and refocussed.

When we write we have to compose and order our thoughts, and many teachers have become more aware of the way that writing can engage thinking and deepen reflective thought; in other words, they have become more aware of the cognitive processes in writing. Scardamalia and Bereiter's research into composing processes (1985) addresses the question of how writing enhances knowledge, and brings about different kinds of thinking. They argue that writing involves the creation of a synthesis between what the writer wants to say on the one hand, and textual constraints on the other. They explore the inevitable tension between handling the content and the audience.

Understanding young children's writing

A process approach is not restricted to relatively competent young writers. Children in the very early stages of learning to write can benefit from an approach which recognises that they have intentions as writers, that they are active in the process they are learning, and that through writing they are learning about the world and how to represent it in written language. In the last twenty years, the practice of tracing, then copying the teacher's writing, and then constructing simple sentences from key words, has become less common. Teachers have become more aware of what Teale and Sulzby (after Marie Clay, see Chapter 1) call 'emergent literacy'. Teale and Sulzby (1986) argue that emergent is a significant term because 'it connotes development rather than stasis' and that as researchers have looked increasingly closely at literacy learning in very young children, they have come to the conclusion that . . . it is not reasonable to point to a time in a child's life when literacy begins. Rather, at whatever point we look, we see children in the process of becoming literate, as the term implies' (Teale and Sulzby, 1986; p. xxv).

Emergent writing (sometimes known as 'developmental' writing, see Chapter 5) is an aspect of emergent literacy. An emergent writing approach recognises that children know a good deal about writing from a very early age. As we saw in Chapter 1, the marks children make represent meaning, and what parents often describe as scribbles are more often patiently and painstakingly constructed communications, as children learn both that language is a symbolic system for expressing meaning and that it has rules of usage. Perhaps the key point about emergent writing is that the writing is 'for real', not a rehearsal for proper writing later, or a series of actions to be practised for when the real writing starts. Children are active 'meaning makers' (Wells, 1987), a view of the learner which is very different from that of the passive child copying letters.

An emergent writing approach encourages creativity and invention: it frees children from the fear and constraint of making mistakes and encourages them to experiment and to feel successful in what they have produced. The teacher can then respond to and monitor development as the children begin to learn about the writing system. For example, teachers can see that children's invented spellings are logical and can recognise the strategies the children use as they move through the developmental stages of spelling, from 'pre-communicative', where there is an imperfect match between sound and written symbol, to more or less fully accurate spelling (Gentry, 1982 and see Chapter 5 of this volume). In an emergent writing approach, children are encouraged to hypothesise about spelling rather than relying on spellings given by the teacher. In working out how to represent sounds for themselves, phonemic awareness, a key skill in learning to read, is developed (see Adams, 1990 and Chapter 5 in this book). Teachers can also see how children handle the grammatical aspects of writing and can monitor children's development and support them in moving onto the next stage, so that the children are learning transcription through composition, the skills through the process as a whole, rather than focussing on the skills first.

An emergent writing approach accepts that writing does not start and end at the classroom door. Teachers today are more aware than in the past of the importance of children's cultural backgrounds and experiences and of the need to build on these educationally. In terms of writing, it means that teachers recognise that children already exhibit literate behaviours, that they are aware of some of the functions of writing and that they come from families and communities where writing is thought of and used in particular ways.

Understanding about cultural and linguistic differences

In school, particular kinds of writing are taught. Outside school, different social and cultural groups will have different attitudes to, and different ways of using, writing, some of which will accord with schooled practices and some of which may even be in conflict with them. For example, Street (1995) describes Philadelphian adolescents with empty exercise books in school but notebooks and scrapbooks full of things like raps and messages out of school. These young people have resisted the kinds of writing the school values and have forged their own uses for writing and forms of writing outside school, raising interesting issues about the approach taken by the school.

Literacy is often viewed as a neutral technology, a set of skills you just learn to use, but many researchers and teachers argue that it is far from neutral, that literacy involves specific ways of representing knowledge and developing understanding. Some suggest that schooled literacy is too narrow in its conceptualisation of writing and that it inducts children into too limited a range of writing competences. Street (1995), for example, draws a distinction between an autonomous model of literacy, defined as a single, dominant kind of literacy, and an ideological model, which recognises a multiplicity of literacy practices, specific to particular cultural contexts. A number of longitudinal ethnographic studies have examined the interface of these different literacy practices: for example, Heath (1983), in her study of three communities in the United States, examines the nature of these differing literacy events across the communities, demonstrating that the children in each community are inducted into very different literacy practices and learn differently about what writing is for and how it is used. More recently, and in an English context, Barton and Hamilton (1998) have studied the literacy practices of people in Lancaster and draw similar inferences.

So for teachers to 'build' on children's backgrounds means more than asking them about their lives outside school: it means recognising that their literacy knowledge comes both from the school context and the home culture and that their experiences of writing will not be uniform. The teacher therefore needs to value and nurture the types of writing done at home, at the same time as introducing children to the kinds of writing done in school (see Chapter 3 for a discussion of links between home and school).

A recognition of home literacy practices is particularly important for children for whom English is an additional language (EAL). For these children, in the past, special provision separated them from contexts in which they could read, write and speak English naturally. They were taught discrete skills before engaging with real writing. They were treated as though they were starting from scratch in their literacy development, yet many of the children were literate in a language other than English and such practices served only to hold back their development.

Teachers have also become more aware that the needs of bilingual writers are very similar to those of first language writers. In addition, recent developments in understanding of EAL indicate the vital importance socially and cognitively of supporting the first language at the same time as enhancing the additional language, in reading, writing and speaking and listening. For example, Baker (1996, p. 136 and p. 142) analyses research into bilingualism and thinking and concludes that 'the judgement of the clear majority of researchers tends to be that there are positive links between bilingualism and cognitive functioning' and that bilingual children may have an increased communicative sensitivity and increased metalinguistic awareness, that is, understanding of, and sensitivity to, language.

UNDERSTANDING THE NATURE OF WRITTEN LANGUAGE

Alongside developments in understanding the process of writing, there have been significant developments in teachers' and researchers' understanding of writing as a system, of the linguistic characteristics of written language. There are two main ways in which teachers' greater linguistic understanding of language is influencing practice in the teaching of writing.

Spoken and written language

The first area of increasing knowledge about the nature of writing is its relation to other modes of language, particularly to spoken language. Teachers need to understand something of the relation of spoken and written modes of language because, in learning to write, children have to learn to operate in a secondary discourse (speech is the first discourse they learn) and to put their language into written form. If teachers can understand how children are learning to operate in the secondary discourse of writing, they may be better able to understand what the children are trying to convey and to discuss differences in spoken and written language with them.

Speech and writing clearly differ in their processes: speech is more context dependent; usually takes place face to face, so is more interactive; can use all the resources of body language, intonation and volume; and is characterised by false starts, repetitions and hesitations. Written language must convey its meanings without face to face contact; must be more explicit; is usually non-interactive, more planned and less spontaneous; and relies on punctuation and other written features such as capitalisation or fonts to make its effects. Writers have to predict responses or misunderstandings and must be much more aware of the needs of the reader.

There is, however, a danger in thinking that speech and writing are totally different systems. Sometimes speech can be like writing, as in a formal lecture or public speech, which would be more like written language than speech. Similarly, some writing is very like speech, such as personal correspondence or messages on notepads. The important point here is that children need to understand that the purpose of the writing, and its intended audience, will determine the level of formality of the writing and that this in turn will determine the form of the writing.

There is a good deal of evidence to indicate that speech and writing also have different grammatical and syntactical organisation. Information units are bundled, or 'chunked', differently in speech and writing. In speech, the main linguistic unit is the clause. In writing, clauses are connected and related to each other into sentences, then sentences are linked into paragraphs and so on. Basically, sentences are made from clauses and the task facing the writer is how to connect the ideas in the clauses. Writing, therefore, requires decisions about what the main ideas are, what is subsidiary, in which order to place things, and which information is subordinate to the main information units of the sentence.

In relation to continuous prose, a reader can revisit what has been read to check any misunderstanding or to follow a line of thought, so the structure can be relatively complex. In speech, the communication is more linear and transient and a listener cannot keep checking what has been said, unless through repeated interruptions. So learning to write involves both developing control over the sentence and learning to be more explicit, and linguistic research can provide useful insights into these aspects of writing development. For example, Kress (1982) charts the development of control of the sentence in children's writing and argues that apparent irregularities or mistakes can be viewed differently by teachers once they understand how the child is moving from a spoken to a written mode of thought. Perera's research (1989) into whether children write as they speak, as is often suggested, found that this was not actually the case. Children increasingly edit out typical speech forms from their writing as they become more familiar with written language, demonstrating the importance of reading to writing development.

For many children, learning to write means adding Standard English to their repertoire. Writing is almost always conducted in Standard English, though the style, register, and genre will differ, whereas spoken language could be in the standard or another dialect. Teachers need to understand that as well as moving from spoken to written mode, children may be having to make sense of standard written English forms too.

Writing is also related to reading and teachers have become more aware of the models for writing provided by children's reading, not just at the level of the content, or genre, but also at the syntactic level, where children absorb structures for writing. This is one of the reasons why it is important for children to hear written language read aloud which is more challenging than they could read alone. The written language which children hear then provides a resource for their own grammatical and syntactical composing.

Genre theory

The second area of linguistic knowledge which has begun to have an impact on practice is that of a genre-based approach to teaching writing, or genre theory as it is also called. This involves identifying the language features and structures of a range of written texts and teaching them.

Essentially, different types of writing have recognisable patterns of structural organisation and linguistic features. Genres are socially recognised text types (though precise definitions vary somewhat) and the argument is that in teaching writing, generic forms should be explicitly taught. Research in the 1970s carried out by Halliday on behalf of the Schools' Council, and continued in the 1980s and 1990s in Australia by Martin *et al.* (1987), among others, looked at the teaching of English in the context of developments in linguistics. In its later stages, and in relation to writing development, their research involved the extensive collection and analysis of writing done in school. They identified a small range of genres as predominant, yet found that little attention was given to the structure and linguistic content of these genres in the teaching context. In other words, the range of writing experiences the children were having was limited and little attempt was made to explain to children how certain kinds of texts are structured and what their characteristics are. In a British context, similar concerns have been raised about the kinds of writing done in school. In the more distant past, the Plowden Report (DES, 1967) was very critical of the amount of story writing done in primary schools and similar concerns were raised in two further HMI reports (DES, 1978; DES, 1982), which found in primary schools inspected a good deal of copying, much use of exercises in text books and, in terms of the range of types of writing carried out in school, a predominance of personal expressive writing and story writing. Later, in 1993, OFSTED found little had changed: inspection evidence indicated 'excessive copying and a lack of demand for sustained, independent and extended writing' (OFSTED, 1993; p. 8).

The genre theorists identified a number of principal genres, though, as already indicated, many children were experiencing only a small number of these text types. The main genres are described as: recount (chronologically ordered retelling of events: 'last week I went to my nan's'); report (classificatory descriptions of processes and things: 'whales are mammals'); procedure (explanations about how something is done: 'the first player throws the dice'); explanations (of how something works or why something occurs: 'the sea causes the pebbles to move up the beach'); discussion (argument from a range of perspectives with conclusion: 'should fox-hunting be banned?'); persuasion (persuasive writing promoting one point of view: 'I think fox-hunting should be banned'); and narrative ('there was once a village where nobody grew old'). In early writing, other common genres are identified, such as labelling ('this is my teddy') and labelling/observation ('this is my teddy and I love him').

Whether this is a sufficiently inclusive list is an interesting question, but it does reflect the *National Curriculum* requirement for range in writing. The main question and contentious issue in genre-based approaches is to what extent the teaching should be explicit about specific linguistic features of texts and what the pedagogical implications are of direct teaching about linguistic forms. Most teachers feel reasonably comfortable talking about the audience for a piece of writing and how this will shape the language used, such as formal or informal, or the general form of the writing. However, beyond this, at the more detailed linguistic level, such as the type of verb used in a particular genre, or the implied question and answer structure of newspaper journalism, many teachers feel less secure and sometimes quite out of their depth. Lewis and Wray (1995) report from their research into teachers' practices in teaching writing that, when asked about writing, 'most teachers tended to concentrate their replies on the writing of narrative texts' and that there was:

> a general lack of knowledge of the range of texts, and at the least, a lack of a shared vocabulary with which to discuss text types. (The research) supports the hypothesis of Ofsted, that teachers need to improve their own knowledge about the 'structures, functions and variations' of language.
> (p. 11)

We might expect teachers to be more confident in the area of narrative, a common enough feature of primary writing, but even the writing of narrative receives little support in terms of the explicit teaching of generic features. In fact, the term 'story' is often used to refer to both narratives and recounts and for some children writing a story means writing a recount, rather than an actual narrative, with stages such as orientation and complication (see Chapter 4). Recounts are by far the most common genre in primary schools, which raises questions about whether children are experiencing the necessary range, particularly in relation to the requirements of the National Curriculum. Genre theorists argue that the narrow range of writing done in school should be extended to prepare children to write more socially relevant genres, so that writing is more meaningful in the 'real' world, though they also recognise that certain kinds of writing are expected in the curriculum and the formal examination system and must be taught. Teachers should be trying to get a better balance in terms of other genres identified by the genre theorists, but this is also problematic: for example, Barrs (1994) argues that the main problem with what the theory advocates is that it does not relate well to what we know of children's development as writers. Most writing by children, she says, mixes genres and does not reflect the kinds of genres identified by linguists. Such genres should not be deemed 'failed adult genres', but developmental genres in their own right. To expect children to write specific structures, and to expect teachers to adopt codified rules for writing, stifles writing development and is inappropriate in the primary classroom.

Genre theory purports to be a social theory of writing development because it identifies and teaches kinds of writing which are more significant in the world than the narrow diet of writing many children experience in school. What children learn to write, as well as how they learn, becomes an issue of entitlement and empowerment. How teachers move forward on this will depend on their view of the purposes of writing, and their understanding of the linguistic issues involved.

Despite these contentious areas, greater attention to genre is emerging in British primary classrooms. Research is urgently needed into the level of knowledge teachers and children need and the methodologies for teaching genres. One example of a such a methodology comes from the work of Lewis and Wray (1995) on writing frames in non-fiction. Writing frames are outline structures for different generic forms which Lewis and Wray analyse and implement with primary children (see Chapter 4 for a more detailed discussion of supportive structures for writing).

CONTROVERSY IN THE TEACHING OF WRITING

Writing has, for a long time, been a controversial aspect of education, because people have differing views about what counts as being literate. Lay and professional views often come into conflict and writing is in the firing line because it is more tangible than reading: employers, for example, actually see writing, whereas weaknesses in reading are less visible. Standards of literacy, in terms of writing, focus almost exclusively on transcriptional aspects and on the grammatical aspects of composition (and on narrow aspects of each) and public judgements on these are widely reported in the media. Whether standards are declining is a very complex matter, partly because of the problem of the validity of comparative studies of standards in writing: the measures to be used, the changing demands on writing, the scale of the sample and its replicability all serve to make comparisons across time difficult. The assessment required in the *National Curriculum* may enable better comparisons to be drawn in the future, but even this national data will not necessarily give a full picture of writing standards, other than in relation to transcription. As Brian Cox (1991), chair of the group which proposed the curriculum and assessment for English in the *National Curriculum*, remarks, 'the best writing is vigorous, committed, honest and interesting. We did not include these qualities in our statements of attainment because they cannot be mapped onto levels' (p. 147).

In terms of pedagogy, writing is controversial because of debates about what children need to know about language: the question is whether children need to know about the forms of the English language in order to be able to write, or whether knowledge about forms emerges through writing. Knowledge about language has been seen as important for children in several government reports (DES, 1984; DES, 1988; DES, 1989) and the *National Curriculum* included this area under 'Standard English and Language Study'. There was always a concern that separate, decontextualised language teaching would be insisted upon and that a more holistic and process approach to language development would be ignored. However, an insistence on drills and exercises has not emerged: for example, there is a definite intention in the

National Literacy Strategy (see below) to ensure that children's knowledge about language is contextualised in their own reading and writing and that learning about the forms of the English language arises from meaningful contexts.

TOWARDS THE TURN OF THE CENTURY

The last twenty years have seen considerable changes in the teaching of writing. Some of these have arisen from research and publications which have influenced practice. Some have been centrally sponsored, such as the *National Writing Project* (1985–9), which established major regional networks of groups looking into aspects of writing. Teachers conducted action research into writing development in all areas of the curriculum and across all age phases; they published materials and newsletters about their work on writing and raised the profile of writing in schools in a way which is still influential today. At the end of the 1990s, a rather different approach can be seen. The *National Literacy Strategy* is taking hold in primary schools, setting a revised and refocussed agenda for the teaching of reading and writing. Its Framework for Teaching prescribes a syllabus for reading and writing for short- and long-term planning and specifies the orientation of a daily hour of explicit literacy teaching (the Literacy Hour), which requires 'systematic, regular and frequent' teaching of discrete aspects of language such as phonological awareness, phonics, spelling, grammar and punctuation. The *NLS* is part of the government's drive to raise literacy standards and to achieve the target of 80 per cent of 11 year olds achieving level 4 or above in Key Stage 2 English tests by 2001, an ambitious target requiring major financial investment.

Now information and communications technology (ICT) brings even greater challenges for the teaching and learning of writing, with new technologies for writing and new genres to be learned. Word-processing offers immense possibilities for writing development: Graves' model for writing becomes more manageable through the applications of ICT, particularly in relation to editing, proofreading and publishing. Manual transcription may soon be seen as less important than the development of keyboard skills, even in very young children, though the resource and training implications are considerable. The national networking of schools opens up significant opportunities for new audiences for writing, new kinds of information texts to be read, and new ways of sending and receiving writing.

The turn of the century sees the teaching of writing once again under scrutiny. More than ever, teachers need to feel that they have writing 'under control', and are secure in what they do to develop children as writers, so that the best of the past can combine with the new initiatives of today.

Further reading

Cox, B. (1991) *Cox on Cox, An English Curriculum for the 1990s*. Sevenoaks: Hodder and Stoughton.
Graves, D. (1983) *Writing: Teachers and Children at Work*. New Hampshire: Heinemann.
National Writing Project (1990) *Perceptions of Writing*. Surrey: Nelson.

CHAPTER 3

Routines and Resources

Anne Washtell

> Miss, you hold my hand and show me how to write.
> (Katrina, 5.0)

INTRODUCTION

These words, spoken in frustration by an inexperienced young writer, indicate the crucial and central role of the teacher in enabling children to succeed as they begin to take control of writing. In order to provide effective support, we must establish a set of regular, well understood, purposeful classroom writing routines which will permit the understanding of all elements of the writing process to develop.

In this chapter, we look at a selection of commonly used writing routines, some or all of which you are likely to find in your classroom. Most of the routines that are discussed here are related to the compositional side of writing although, inevitably, there will be an overlap with spelling, handwriting and punctuation. As each writing routine is discussed, it will be linked, where appropriate, to the *English National Curriculum* (DfEE, 1995) Programmes of Study for writing, the *NLS* and the *Desirable Outcomes* document (SCAA, 1996a), and a clear indication of suitability to particular age ranges will also be given.

What are writing routines and why do we need them? Writing routines are strategies and skills that underpin the various elements of the writing process. Some routines need to be at the level of regular practice, such as copying and tracing in the early years, whereas others, for example, shared writing, are used by the teacher to make aspects of the process explicit to the children prior to independent activity (for example, when using writing frames). We need to provide children with a well balanced range of writing routines in order that they do not become over-reliant on a narrow field of strategies and skills at the expense of others. Limited provision of routines by the teacher could lead to serious weaknesses and ultimately difficulties in the children's development and growing independence as writers. Therefore, building a selection of writing routines into medium- and short-term planning is essential. If we do not think carefully about writing routines at the point of planning, we cannot guarantee balance and variety in terms of the strategies and skills that we want to encourage children to use.

PLANNING FOR WRITING ROUTINES

Before planning your writing routines, it is important to read the school's agreed policy on writing as you may find that particular routines, approaches and resources are specified and targeted in specific age ranges. In addition, the school will have a long-term plan which will provide further detailed information about the progression of skills and genres of writing to be taught as the children move up through the school. This information is frequently documented on a term by term basis, year group by year group and is intended to form the framework from which teachers write their medium-term plans (also known as Schemes of Work). It is helpful when writing medium-term plans to think about the three types of planning identified by SCAA (1995b) and central to the *NLS* (DfEE, 1998b): these are 'blocked', 'linked' and 'continuous'. Blocked planning essentially describes a discrete unit of pure English work, for example, in Key Stage Two, a series of lessons over a period of four weeks to develop children's knowledge of the linguistic features of writing argument and persuasion. Linked planning, as its name suggests, involves linking writing to another area of the curriculum to provide purposeful writing in a range of genres. An example of this might be a history topic such as World War Two where the class might undertake writing in various genres, for example, diary and report writing (see Chapter 4). Continuous planning (sometimes known as 'drip-feed') includes important routines which require regular practice, week in, week out, an example being handwriting (see Chapter 5).

By referring to the statutory documentation at this planning stage, you can clarify learning intentions and outcomes and ensure that your work is pitched at the appropriate level(s). Short-term plans (usually on a weekly basis) expand the material contained in the medium-term plans. Decisions about differentiation within the activities will also be made at this stage, based on previous observations and assessments. For example, it might be appropriate for a child who is struggling with writing to have his/her story scribed by an adult.

The Literacy Hour

Another factor which will have an increasing impact on planning for writing is the Literacy Hour initiative. It is underpinned by a detailed document entitled *The National Literacy Strategy: Framework for Teaching* (DfEE, 1998b). This Framework details year group by year group (from Reception to Year 6), term by term, a set of teaching objectives to enable teachers to implement the Literacy Hour with maximum efficiency. The intention behind the Framework is to ensure that all teachers have high expectations of their pupils and that children's experience in literacy follows a clearly defined, progressive and well balanced sequence. It is not necessary to go into further detail as the *NLS* framework does this for you.

In the *NLS*, writing, like reading, is intended to take place at Text, Sentence and Word level. The Framework allows for a balance between writing which is 'modelled' (where the teacher takes responsibility through demonstration) and independent writing (where the child takes responsibility for his/her writing). The first fifteen minutes, which is dedicated to whole-class teaching, is used by the teacher for shared reading and shared writing. Still working with the whole class, the next fifteen minutes are spent mainly on word level work in Key Stage One and a balance of Word and Sentence level work in Key Stage Two. The third phase (which lasts for twenty minutes) of the Literacy Hour shifts the emphasis to group activity with the teacher providing guided text work (which can be reading or writing) with two focus groups per day, and three groups working independently. It is very important, in the early days of working with the Literacy Hour, that you establish a set of clearly defined 'self-help' routines with your class in order to help those groups work independently. We look at some self-help routines later in this chapter. The final ten minutes of the Literacy Hour, the 'plenary', provide an opportunity for the children to report back and reflect on their work and for teaching points to be consolidated.

The *NLS* document lists the many aspects of the writing process which will be taught and also makes clear, in its rationale on guided writing and independent work, that there is a very particular purpose behind the writing activities. 'These sessions should also be used to meet specific objectives and focus on specific aspects of the writing process,' (DfEE, 1998, p. 12). Because such writing sessions will necessarily be quite short, it will be important to sustain children's enthusiasm for writing outside the hour as well. This can be done in Reception by making provision for writing and other forms of representation through children's play activities, and routines such as dictated writing allow the child to compose a complete piece of work. In Key Stages One and Two, opportunities for writing outside the Literacy Hour can be identified through linked planning (discussed above) and also by making provision for sustained periods of time where children can write, uninterrupted, and at length.

SHARED WRITING

I first heard the term 'shared writing' in the mid-1980s. It was used by teachers and staff attending courses in London at the Centre For Language in Primary Education (CLPE). Shared writing was the natural development from another literacy routine known as 'shared reading'. Shared reading's roots can be traced to New Zealand and the work of Don Holdaway (1979) whose ideas were based on what he described as 'the bed-time story cycle' where certain characteristic routines (including returning to familiar texts and engaging in highly interactive dialogue) regularly took place between parents and children as they shared books. He felt that this experience was so enriching for children that it could be replicated in the classroom by means of enlarged texts. Through the use of big books, the whole class or groups of children can learn collaboratively about any aspect of the reading or writing process that the teacher chooses to focus on. The teacher takes the lead and 'scaffolds' (to borrow Bruner's term, 1976, in Wood *et al.*, p. 63) the children's learning by modelling skills and strategies that s/he wishes the children to experience and learn for later independent use. Through explicit and highly interactive teaching the children are introduced to new areas of learning but they also revisit and consolidate previous experiences. Most importantly, through the collaborative nature of shared reading and/or writing, the teacher can set high expectations by placing the children in what Vygotsky (1978) calls 'the zone of proximal development' (see Chapter 1). In so doing, the children are led into fresh areas of knowledge and skills that they cannot yet undertake independently.

Shared writing can be undertaken with any age range and can be used for short tasks or more extended pieces of work. The teacher acts as scribe (i.e. s/he does the writing), thus freeing the children to participate fully in the creation of the text and to learn about the writing process from an experienced writer. In order for this to be effective, we need to be clear about our teaching objective(s) for each session and to make sure that we provide an explanatory commentary as we write. It is important to ask the children searching questions which relate to our teaching objective(s) and to encourage interactive responses. By listening to children's responses, we can attune ourselves to their current conceptual understanding or misconceptions about the writing process and differentiate further questions accordingly. For example, in response to the question, "Where should I start writing?" a child might point to the bottom of the piece of paper. Noting the child's misconception, the teacher might then ask the same child a more closed question such as, "Can you point to the top of the page and show me where to start writing?". We can also encourage the children to take on specific, previously introduced terminology, such as 'verb', 'paragraph' or 'speech marks'; this develops their use of metalanguage (a language with which to talk about language) by framing questions in such a way that they are required to try to use the terminology in their answers and explanations.

This 'talking about writing' is crucial for children if they are to make the move from dependence to independence as writers and as they begin to learn how to make explicit their implicit knowledge about how written language works. These collaborative opportunities to reflect on the writing process will be especially supportive to those children who have learning difficulties and also for those in the early stages of learning English. Some children will be listening to and absorbing knowledge and it may take time before they feel confident enough to share their ideas with the whole class.

Successful shared writing in the Nursery and Reception classes is often based on simple rewriting of well known predictable texts. In a Reception class we took a favourite book, *The Monsters' Party* (Story Chest, 1980), and rewrote it as *The Nice Monsters' Party*. The pattern of the story was simple: 'What can this nice monster do? He can dance, that's what he can do.' We substituted new action words, such as 'leap' for 'dance', and invented a surprise ending for the story which went as follows: 'What can I do? I can jump in the cake like a kangaroo.' The draft was reproduced as a big book, illustrated by the children and reread many times. The children also re-enacted the book in role play. At Text level the activity provided a model of a simple narrative structure and at Sentence level it drew attention to the idea of questions and how we punctuate them. At Word level we had looked closely at alternative action words (verbs).

It is not difficult to provide a real purpose for shared writing with young children and contexts can arise from everyday events. In a Reception class, a child suddenly left the school midway through the term. The children wanted to send her a message in the form of a big poster. Through shared writing I scribed the short and simple message, 'We love you so much Katrina.' Having reread the message together through shared reading, the children spontaneously began to play at spotting the letters of their names in the text. This proved an exciting and intense activity which lasted for approximately ten minutes with everyone participating at increasing levels of complexity. I include this example as a reminder that children are as capable as teachers at initiating purposeful opportunities for learning. In this very young age group, the skill of playing with and manipulating language must be nurtured and encouraged.

Shared writing is a flexible teaching tool to use with children. It can support any aspect of composition and transcription. In Key Stage Two, it can be used to model the linguistic features of more challenging writing genres, such as arguments or reports (see Chapter 4 on writing frames). In Key Stage Two, shared writing can also be very effective in teaching children skills which we as adults may take for granted. One such skill is that of note taking. Through the shared reading of an enlarged extract from an information text, the teacher can demonstrate how to use the skills of skimming and scanning to extract information, listing key words and points. Useful strategies and techniques can be demonstrated, such as using simple abbreviations which can speed up the note-taking process. For example, when writing notes about the Gunpowder Plot, a teacher demonstrated to the class how to use the initials of the conspirators rather than writing their names out in full. So, Guy Fawkes became 'G.F.' and Robert Catesby 'R.C.' (A similar example is given in Chapter 5 but this time in the first draft of a child's independent writing.) To read more about teaching note taking see Chapter 4.

When resourcing shared writing, most teachers prefer to work with a flip chart and felt pens; alternatively, you could use the board or an acetate on the overhead projector. The size and appearance of your handwriting is a further consideration, especially if children are seated at some distance from you.

It is important that a proportion of the shared writing drafts are reproduced as finished products. The type of product will be determined by the type of text being produced. For example, a story text could be reproduced into a home-made big book which the children go on to illustrate and reread. Other texts will become posters, captions, sentences or word lists to go on the wall. Some material will be word-processed.

To conclude, shared writing can be used to model any of the following:

- A sense of purpose and audience: voice (formal or informal); planning; drafting; revising; proofreading; presentation (publication).
- Content and features of different types of texts: linguistic features; structural features; vocabulary choices for specific genres; grammatical features.
- Transcription skills: punctuation; spelling; handwriting.
- Self-help strategies: correcting mistakes; discussing; peer conferencing; collaborating; use of resources.

COLLABORATIVE WRITING

In this routine, children work together, independently of the teacher, to produce a shared written text. The text could be written on a large piece of paper or composed on screen. As it requires a high level of co operation, collaborative writing is best suited to the top end of Key Stage One and to Key Stage Two. For children to succeed in this writing routine, the groups should be small (preferably even numbers) and carefully constructed to ensure compatibility. The ground rules for participation should also be clearly explained and, ideally, everyone in the group should take a turn to write with the mutual support of the other group members. This activity can work very effectively as part of the Literacy Hour. A Year 2 class had listened to a rereading of a story in the first part of the Literacy Hour and had been asked to retell the story orally in their groups and then rewrite the main sequence of events to accompany a set of pictures. The pictures had already been sequenced and stuck on to a large piece of paper in the previous session and the children's main task was to compose and then write their sentence to accompany each illustration. This independent writing group supported one another, taking turns to suggest possible sentences, agreeing on the best one and then working in pairs to write the sentences down. The children who were waiting for their turn to write, either helped with suggestions for spellings or wrote a rough draft of their sentence on small pieces of paper. In the plenary session, the group read their story aloud to the rest of the class.

DICTATED WRITING

A five year old told me a wonderful story which was full of vivid description and interesting twists of plot. She told me her story was in chapters. When she had finished telling me the story, I asked her to write it down. Slowly and laboriously she managed to write one sentence, 'I love my dog.' She stopped in dismay, saying, 'I've done my best' and I, as her teacher, was also left feeling disappointed. Between the two of us, we had lost that wonderful story. This example will probably sound familiar to many teachers of young children and I include it here to illustrate the gap between the child's potential competence as an author and her performance as a writer. As a result of years of being told and read stories at home, this child was a skilled 'author' but she was also a very inexperienced writer in terms of the 'secretarial' skills (i.e. knowledge about the spelling and handwriting system, see Chapter 2). For this child and many others like her, dictated writing is an important routine as it maintains, sustains and develops the child's skills as an author while the child begins to come to grips with the physical aspects of the writing process. Dictated writing, as its name suggests, involves the teacher (or other adult) working on a one-to-one basis with a child in order to scribe for the child. It is a labour-intensive routine, but teachers are surprised and delighted not only by the extended pieces of writing that can result, but also by the complexity of the language structures used and the richness of vocabulary. You may at this stage want to look back at the 'dogfish' example we gave in the introduction.

Liz Laycock (1996) provides a detailed account of several young children and their dictated stories. She reminds us that to create and tell stories is a very human activity: 'In telling our stories, putting our fears, doubts, excitements, joys or sorrows into words, we are shaping them in order to make sense of them, both for ourselves and for the listeners' (Laycock, 1996; p. 54). This may in part explain why this writing routine is so popular with many young children. She analyses the narrative structure of stories dictated by children in a Reception class showing that such young children already know a great deal about how narratives are constructed.

Although dictated writing is usually thought of as an early years routine, it is acknowledged in the Key Stage One Programme of Study for writing that occasionally it will be appropriate for teachers to scribe for children to 'help pupils compose at greater length . . . demonstrating the ways that ideas may be recorded in print (p. 9)'. This routine also has considerable potential for children who are in difficulties with writing or who are disaffected by writing. For this reason, children may be asked to tape stories in Key Stage Two for the teacher to transcribe for them later on (see Chapter 7). Whatever the age range, dictated writing can be turned into valuable reading material for the children.

TEACHER DICTATING TO THE CLASS

'Dictation' has a rather old-fashioned tone, but one Year 5 teacher has a successful continuous routine called 'You are my secretaries'. On one occasion the class had been writing letters of complaint and the teacher decided to read them a letter she had composed to provide a further model of the linguistic features of the genre. She then asked them to 'take a letter' and dictated a short passage to the children. This was followed by pair or group work where the children compared the versions that they had written down and then they extended these to produce a final version. The plenary session was then used to read out and defend their versions. Ruth Wajnryb (1990) has developed a method of dictation to young children which is also suitable for EAL children where she reads a passage to her listeners several times with the children noting down as many words each time as possible. In pairs the children then attempt to reconstruct the whole text.

Although dictation is not mentioned in the Programme of Study, many teachers find it a useful routine to use occasionally, especially when they are trying to gain direct feedback on a particular aspect of the child's knowledge of the writing process. Dictation, in its traditional form, places heavy, simultaneous demands on the child's working knowledge of the writing system. These days, teachers may choose to use the technique rather more flexibly than the nineteenth century teacher in the Introduction to this book. For instance, the teacher might use it to consolidate a specific teaching point on spelling which would take the form of dictating a short, specially tailored piece of writing rather than a lengthy stretch of text which tested everything. In this way, teachers could reinforce points about genre, sentence structure, punctuation, paragraphing, layout, spelling and handwriting.

COPYING AND TRACING

As with the previous routine, copying and tracing have had a long and at times controversial history (see Introduction and Chapter 1), especially in terms of their overuse at the expense of those other routines which place more emphasis on the active participation and hypothesising of the child. However, these copying and tracing routines are still commonly practised in early years classrooms, and with some children in Key Stage One who might still benefit from them. They are important routines for several reasons: they help in the child's physical development by improving hand/eye coordination and by providing opportunities to refine the child's fine motor skills; they play their part in developing the child's growing awareness of print by drawing his or her attention to key concepts about print; children seem to benefit from the time that these routines give them to reflect on their writing and they love the neat end product!

Go into any children's bookshop and you will see plenty of attractively produced, graded, exercise books that focus on copying and tracing. The tracing activities teach children about directionality and familiarise children with the key movements that underpin handwriting and letter formation. The task is made achievable for the child by virtue of tracing on top of a 'good model' of the particular pattern to be practised. It could then be argued that through tracing the child gets a 'feel' for handwriting (see Handwriting in Chapter 5).

In early years classrooms, teachers will plan, at a continuous level, a variety of tracing-related activities to help children practise the necessary skills involved in learning how to hold and control a writing implement. The child may trace over a wide range of pre-drawn outlines of everyday objects and shapes. Literacy related tracing activities will include tracing over handwriting patterns, tracing over individual letters of the alphabet to develop knowledge of shape and orientation and, most significantly, tracing over the child's name. Kinaesthetic provision will also be made for independent experiences arising from tracing, such as, writing in wet sand, tracing the finger over raised letters, or finger painting. Some of the routines described here are also used with older children with serious literacy and fine motor difficulties (see also Chapter 7).

For many children, copying marks the first stage towards independent handwriting. The first word that most children copy, with some degree of accuracy, is their name. Through name writing they will begin to develop an awareness that letters can be written in both upper and lower case. The *Desirable Outcomes* (SCAA, 1996a) expects children to recognise the letters of the alphabet by shape and sound. They are also expected to write their names 'with appropriate use of upper and lower case letters'. By participating in a range of the routines discussed above, young children can begin to develop this knowledge. It is important to talk with children when they undertake these tasks in order to find out what they find easy and difficult about the activities. Copying and tracing without teacher intervention tend to be very passive activities and, therefore, less useful.

Another common practice in early years classrooms is to ask the child to compose a sentence which the teacher writes down. Then the child copies underneath. It is important to offer a good model of handwriting and to remind children who are new to copying where to start writing. This could be done by marking the appropriate starting point on their page with a dot. You may find that some children try to write over your writing or copy words, or indeed letters, out of sequence. A Reception class teacher who observed this decided to introduce a midway step which she called 'overwriting'. In this procedure, instead of copying underneath, the child overwrites the teacher's handwriting. This forms a bridge between tracing and copying. The quotation from Katrina at the beginning of this chapter underlines the value of this kind of support.

Children meet a wide range of other forms of copying in the course of a day. If the children are using *Breakthrough to Literacy* (McKay, 1970) they may be asked to copy the sentences which they have made from word cards taken from their sentence makers. The sentences that are written are then intended to become part of the child's reading material.

In Key Stage One, the demands on copying rapidly widen as children will be beginning to copy words from books, including dictionaries or class word banks. They may also be copying work from the board which, in Key Stage Two, becomes an increasingly important routine. To make this workable for children, check that all the children are seated so that they can see the board properly and are comfortable. As with shared writing, your handwriting must be large and clear and, where necessary, cursive. If the children are copying a list such as spellings, where accuracy is vital, make sure that no errors have occurred during the copying. Remember, it is a long distance from the board to the child's book and consider the act of memory involved in maintaining and holding on to the correct letter order. Try to discourage children from copying spellings one letter at a time (see Chapter 5 on developing visual spelling strategies). As accuracy is so important, it may well mean that you need to check the children's books after they have copied the list down. For some children, who have limited short-term memory spans, this kind of copying may prove too demanding. You may need to make other provision, for example, writing the list down for them, in order to support them appropriately. The time may not be far off when you write on an 'interactive whiteboard' and the children are instantly able to download your writing directly onto the personal laptops. The report on this in the *Guardian* (20 May 1998) suggests that pupils will thus be able to avoid 'laborious amounts of copying'. There may be losses, as I have shown that manual copying has a part to play in learning about writing.

In both Key Stage One and Key Stage Two, making fair copies of drafted writing marks the final stage in the writing process. The Key Stage Two Programmes of Study for writing state that children should 'prepare a neat, correct and clear final copy' (DfEE, 1995, p. 15). Children may well be working from drafts that have been revised and edited and may need motivating to put in the final bit of effort. An awareness of the ultimate destination of the final copy will provide an incentive for the children, as will the provision of good quality paper and writing implements with which to execute the task.

INDEPENDENT WRITING

Independent writing (sometimes called 'unaided') involves the child marshalling all of his or her existing knowledge of the writing process in order to produce pieces of writing. In its purest form, as the word implies, the child is expected to write without turning to the teacher for support or referring to resources such as dictionaries. The writing produced may appear unconventional in its appearance, layout and spelling but will provide valuable information about the child's current stage of development and understanding of the writing process. In practice, the teacher will make judgements about interventions and the level of support the child needs in order to succeed but the writing produced will be the result of the child's own efforts. The success of independent writing as a routine rests on the degree of confidence and independence that the young writer has. All children, whatever their age, should have the opportunity and materials to write independently and need to be provided with the strategies to support them in their endeavours. Independent writing features prominently in the Literacy Hour during group work. From the assessment point of view, independent writing is essential as it is only through the child's own written products that we can gain an accurate understanding of his or her current development and thus measure the effectiveness of our teaching. This point is demonstrated by the two pieces of writing in Figures 3.1 and 3.2 by five year old Tommy:

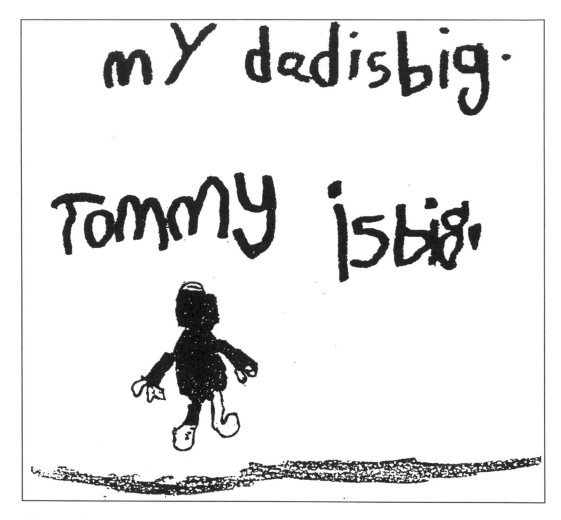

Figure 3.1

The two pieces were written on the same day. Tommy's previous experience had largely come from working with *Breakthrough to Literacy* materials and he had only recently begun to make the move into the unaided writing routine. Both pieces consist of one sentence. The first example (copied from *Breakthrough to Literacy* materials) reveals information about his handwriting and copying skills while the second is written completely unaided and reveals a wider range of information about his understanding of the writing process. The second one reads: 'Danny Farley and I play out'. Figure 3.1 shows that Tommy is able to copy successfully with good control from the printed model provided by the *Breakthrough* materials. In his unaided writing, Figure 3.2, it is immediately noticeable that Tommy's handwriting seems much less controlled. It is bigger and the letter formation is a mix of upper and lower case. However, he does show: an awareness of directionality; an understanding that words must have spaces between them; an appreciation that sentences must end with full stops; and a confidence in trying to spell all the words for himself. These two pieces provide evidence about Tommy's transcription skills but it would be necessary to offer

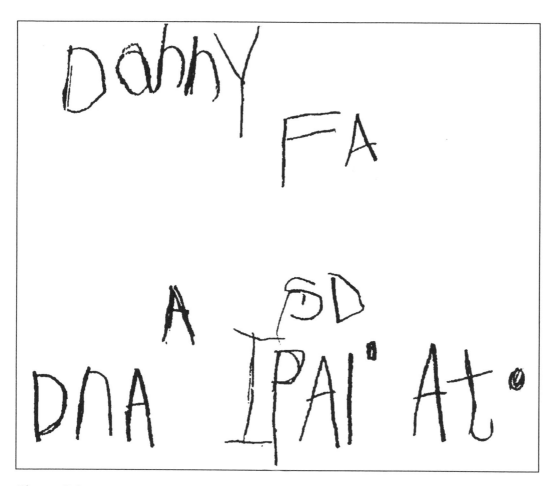

Figure 3.2

other writing routines, such as dictated writing, to form a better impression of his compositional abilities.

Research evidence suggests that from a very early age children are able to write (or communicate meaningfully on paper) for real purposes and audiences. Shirley Payton (1984), in a case study of her daughter Cecelia, provides evidence of the child's early attempts at compiling shopping lists and writing letters to friends. Both Payton and James Britton (1982) show us that very young children want to communicate meaningfully in their writing and will do so initially using non-alphabetic systems of representation. James Britton describes the 'pretend writing' of a young writer explaining how she gradually makes the crucial move from what Vygotsky calls 'drawing objects' to 'drawing speech'. Figure 3.3 provides an example of a very young Reception child's sandwich list compiled in just the same way as her teacher daily compiles a class dinner list.

The list reads, 'Egg sandwich, cheese sandwich, cheese sandwich, cheese sandwich, salad'. A close look at the three central lines reveals that she has represented the words 'cheese sandwich' in a consistent way. Despite its non-alphabetic appearance, the writing is not random but systematic. Such opportunities for self-generated practice are

Figure 3.3

most important in the early years, where children will spontaneously play with the writing system in the way that Marie Clay (1975) describes. The *Desirable Outcomes* also recognises that children will use a variety of means to represent meaning: 'In their writing they use pictures, symbols, familiar words and letters, to communicate meaning, showing awareness of some of the different purposes of writing' (SCAA, 1996).

Resourcing independent writing

Children are not going to be drawn into writing independently unless they have access to resources. Space available varies in classrooms but some kind of central and accessible collection of resources is always possible. A writing area is an incentive and might include some or all of the following resources (depending on the age of the children):

- rough paper
- card and paper (various qualities, colours, sizes, shapes)
- loose-leaf folders
- envelopes and headed notepaper
- blank greetings cards, postcards
- blank official forms to fill in (e.g. travel agent, paying in slips)
- ready-made address books, diaries, birthday books
- material for book covers
- ready-made blank books (variety of qualities)
- book-making material (needles, thread, bookbinding tape)
- boards for book covers, ready-cut blank pages
- clipboards, bulldog clips, paper clips, staplers
- pens, pencils, felt pens, crayons, highlighter pens
- handwriting books, cards, sheets, line guides
- erasers, sharpeners, sellotape, glues, scissors and trimmer
- calligraphy materials, stencils, Letraset.

Additional items might include:

- post box
- notice board and messages board
- easel, large sheets of paper, thick felt pens
- board and chalks
- computer with simple instructions on word-processing packages
- ABC books, alphabet frieze, dictionaries, thesaurus
- display space for children's writing and books
- books such as *The Jolly Postman* (Allan and Janet Ahlberg) and *The Diary of Neil Aitkin* (Cartwright and Campbell).

Displays might include:

- examples of different kinds of writing
- suggestions for starting points for writing
- ideas for drafting

- ideas for finding spellings
- class rules about maintaining the writing area.

(See Chapter 5 for more on transcriptional aspects of the above.)

It is important to look selectively at the above list of ideas in order to provide materials that are suited to the needs of the children. Calligraphy materials, for example, would be aimed at Key Stage Two. Health and safety considerations must also be thought through before resourcing a writing area. Ground rules for use of the resources are also very important, otherwise stock may not be properly used (see the section at the end of this chapter on resources and self-help strategies).

Contexts for independent writing

We also need to provide contexts for purposeful writing activities. It is not uncommon in the early years or Key Stage One to see a writing area or an office set up for the children, or for the home corner to be resourced as a context for role-play and writing. A typical example might be a cafe, where the waiters and waitresses write in role as they take their customers' orders. Older children will also find role-play provides a valuable context for writing and you will find examples of this in Chapter 4.

It is very important that we actively encourage boys to see independent and unaided writing as worthwhile activities for them. Recent evidence from QCA (1998) found that some boys tended to use dedicated writing areas less than girls but responded to role-play areas where the writing was purposeful. We should try to provide writing materials and to create purposes for writing in the areas that boys might prefer to play in. For instance, large posters for writing out safety rules or an order pad used for customers' orders could be part of the large construction area. This is not to say, of course, that boys should not be encouraged to write in the usual writing areas as well.

Responding to independent writing

You may hear children providing a running commentary as they represent their ideas on paper. When children bring us their writing, it helps to raise their awareness about writing as a mode of communication if we encourage them to try to tell us what they think their writing says. In the early stages, their versions may vary from one reading to another which reflects the lack of stability of children's early concepts about print. You may feel that it is appropriate to make a conventional transcription of what children say so that you can refer back to it in future rereadings. A tricky challenge for the inexperienced teacher occurs when the child brings a piece of 'pre-communicative' (see Chapter 2) writing and says, 'You tell me what my writing says'. Such a request is characteristic of some early writers and the teacher can: comment on and name all the different letters that have been used; talk about the use of letters from the child's name in the writing; discuss spaces between words; discuss the length of words; point out repetitions and consistencies. Later, in shared writing or dictated writing she can help the child to make the important connection that print holds meaning.

Confidence and self-help strategies

Children will require a wide range of self-help and self-monitoring strategies in order to sustain their independence and avoid frustration and loss of confidence. Donald Graves (1983) characterises children of seven or eight as moving into a phase where they become very self-conscious as to whether their writing looks right or wrong. Some children by this age are only too aware of their shortcomings, especially in relation to their spelling power. Some children are very fearful of independent writing because it requires them to take risks, thereby making mistakes, and some simply dislike the thought of their writing looking 'messy'. (See discussion on learning styles and strategies for independence in spelling in Chapter 5.) Other children will be struggling with several aspects of learning to write, for example, getting ideas, and will need very achievable short-term goals set to help them (see Chapter 7). You will find self-help ideas at the end of this chapter.

Independent writing is also supportive to children who wish to write on topics that are of particular interest or importance to them, for example a lengthy story in chapters, or an ongoing diary or journal. *The National Curriculum* Programmes of Study in Key Stage One acknowledges this need. Figure 3.4 is a piece of extended writing undertaken independently by a Year 2 writer and indicates the positive benefits of spending a concentrated, uninterrupted period of time drafting a piece of writing.

The child's piece exudes her enthusiasm to recount her adventures and she does this in an entertaining style, for example with the use of parenthesis. She had not been directly taught about brackets but she seizes her opportunity in this piece of writing, using them appropriately, to make a direct address to her reader. For a first draft this example reveals few surface errors but independent writing can also be a very effective way of helping children to learn how to go on to redraft, revise, edit and proofread their writing (skills which they are required to master in Key Stage Two).

DRAFTING

For many years in schools, it was usual for redrafting to be in the form of a 'fair copy'. Bullock *et al.* (1975) makes brief reference to the place of drafting in the classroom but it is through the more recent work of Frank Smith (1982) on the writing process and of Donald Graves (1983) that we have come to a better understanding of what drafting is and its role in the writing process for primary age children. As has already been indicated in Chapter 2, they were concerned that all too often children were being asked to write 'one-off' pieces of writing which tended to lead to an overemphasis on the presentational aspects of writing at the expense of the content. Through his classroom based writing workshops, Graves began to help teachers to see the value of asking children to redraft their work. Central to Graves' approach was to make the whole writing process explicit to children (from pre-composition to publication) and to promote independence in their approach to writing. By the mid-1980s, teachers in this country were encouraging drafting as a routine. For many children this proved to be a liberating experience, although others found it challenging to be asked to redraft their work. In confident hands, the approach worked successfully but it soon became clear that a sense of balance was needed. Questions were raised such as: did every piece of

On the 22nd May Dominique came to my house to stay over night. First Dominique played a game. Then my mum told us to clear up the mess that we had made. Me and Dommique made a model of a dolls house with all the old stuff. Then my mum called and we we had to go upstairs and wash. When we had washed and put on our nightdresses we went downstairs to eat an apple each. We played a game. What you had to do is guess something that begins with a and the second person has to guess something diffrent and the so on and on. Then my mum said it was time to go to bed. So we had to go upstairs to bed. (My guest had my old bed) Just before we got to sleep my Mummy kissed us goodnight. We were asleep in no until we woke up at ten o'clock. We got back to sleep by reading books. In the morning me and Dominique went downstairs and had our breakfast. After breakfast we went upstairs to get dressed. When me and Dominique got in my room we went in the Secret Passage. When we got in we stayed in there for a long time. After half an hour we took our Clothes and went back in the Secret Passage to dress in: to our clothes. After that we Played some games until Louise came to pick her up.

The end

Figure 3.4

writing need to be redrafted? If so, how many times? Wasn't there still a place also for 'one-offs'? Was redrafting necessarily appropriate for all children? Did redrafting entail copying out the complete text again or using editing techniques such as 'cut' and 'paste'? The introduction of the *English National Curriculum* (DfEE, 1995) helped to some extent to clarify the way forward as far as drafting was concerned, placing drafting carefully within a clear progression for producing pieces of writing by requiring children to 'plan', 'draft', 'revise', 'proofread' and 'present' their work.

Some teachers introduce the idea of drafting with younger children through oral redrafting. This can be demonstrated by reading aloud from a short passage of shared writing or from an individual child's own writing and talking about how it could be improved.

Shared writing can also be used to model drafting techniques, including planning, moving paragraphs, marking omissions, changing vocabulary and refining sentence structure. If the children are paired up as 'writing partners' they can support each other with all aspects of drafting, including proofreading. It is also worth teaching the children some basic editor's marks and encouraging them to use them as they draft. Suggested marks include:

- ∧ the omission mark
- circling spelling or alternatively using a wavy or straight line (under a word)
- 'sp.' in the margin to mark spelling errors
- // to indicate a new paragraph is needed.

The word processor is another tool which children can use to assist them in the drafting process. Editing functions such as clicking on 'cut' and 'paste' or dragging across sections of text can assist in the easy movement of paragraphs and sentences while the range of fonts and print sizes provides plenty of scope for the final presentation of pieces of work. However, as the word processor can conceal the different drafts that are produced it is useful for assessment purposes to keep a sample of the 'complete life history' of children's pieces of writing, which shows the progress from initial plan through to the final copy.

Finally, some children want to redraft their work because they can see the value of improving it. Figures 3.5 and 3.6 are from a Year 2 child who speaks English as an Additional Language and show marked developments from first to second draft.

The child wrote Figure 3.5 as a recount of a school trip to the seaside. He became dissatisfied with his work, tried to rub sections out (which accounts for the apparently poor quality of the Figure) and finally asked if he could start again on a fresh piece of paper. Before doing so, we had a brief discussion on the areas that were causing him difficulty and he was given some ideas on improving the content and the sentence structure. This resulted in a second draft, Figure 3.6, which proved a much more satisfying piece of writing. Not only does he add more detail about his trip but he has also tried to regularise his sentence structure and punctuate the piece. There are, of course, still some errors, including confusions over the use of the apostrophe, but the child was much happier with the second draft. For assessment purposes, both drafts provide a wealth of information about the child's growing ability to take control of the writing process and to monitor his own work.

WRITING WORKSHOPS

The idea of the writing workshop comes from Donald Graves (1983) and his research associate Lucy McCormick Calkins (1983). As the name suggests, writing workshops involve the whole class writing together (although not necessarily at the same stage in the writing process). The aim of writing workshops is to make the different stages of

on wednesday the infant
went to the sea-side we
needed three coaches called
blue ways when we go to the
sea-side we had our lunch and
then we went the sea-side we
made and *(illegible)* and then
Doimhis... DaD... took me to thie
(illegible)
(illegible)
(illegible) and
(illegible) and

Figure 3.5

the writing process explicit to children and to enable them to work independently by taking their pieces of writing through from 'pre-composition' to 'publication'. It was intended that children would learn how real writers work by drafting, redrafting, revising, editing and proofreading their pieces, prior to publication. The emphasis of Graves' work was on ownership and children taking an active rather than passive role in their writing.

Teachers who have implemented Graves' model have been impressed at the degree of independence and confidence his approach gives children. They have managed to reduce some of the pressures caused by the mechanics of writing and they have helped children focus more closely on content. While it is unusual to see writing workshops operating in quite these ways today there have been many spin-off practices which we

On wednesday the infant went to the sea-side. We needed three coaches called blue ways when we ways to the seaside wenct I saw 51 apple trees on the way Back. When we and on the sea-side we had our.I got to the we went towards lunch then was covered in sand. Bobby sea-side Gregor when Bobby was covered was covered he had a Flag in sand we went on top of him then an iss - lollipop toilets then we all then we warcht hame

Figure 3.6

almost take for granted these days. These include: 'everyone writing together'; demonstrations or modelling by the teacher; writing response partnerships; talking about the different stages of the process with children; and bookmaking. Publications produced by the National Writing Project (1989–91) describe aspects of good practice which clearly show the influence of Graves' work.

WRITING PARTNERSHIPS

In school, the child's first and most significant writing partner is his or her teacher. It is the teacher who usually provides the first audience and initial response to a piece of writing. The teacher's feedback may also include constructive criticism and guidance on improving the piece of writing. However, as a context for responding, writing partnerships between children can also be very effective and this writing routine is well suited to the Key Stage Two age range. The Programmes of Study, Key Skills 2b states that children should be given the opportunity 'to discuss and evaluate their own and others' writing'. Donald Graves sowed the seeds of writing partnerships through what he termed 'conferencing'. He recommends that conferencing should be a routine part of the drafting process and that initially the teacher should demonstrate to the class how to respond in a positive and constructive way to a piece of writing. He suggests that the teacher start by using one of her own first drafts in order to help the children learn how to respond.

For this routine to work, children need to learn how to ask purposeful and worthwhile questions and how to offer comments in such a way that they do not undermine their partner's confidence. Graves offers two powerful prompts to help children to begin to do this effectively. The first is, 'Tell me something you like about your writing' to be used when the piece is first read aloud. This gives the writer confidence and helps him or her to begin to evaluate the quality of the work. The second prompt, 'Tell me something you want to know more about', is asked by the writer to his or her partner, after the piece has been read aloud. The intention here is to help the children develop their sense of audience by identifying gaps in the writing where more detail or information is required. Ways of operating writing partnerships do vary. Some children are asked to swap their writing, while others read their drafts aloud to one another before their partner responds. The idea is to get the first responses directed towards the content. This could include suggestions for clarifying points, grammatical expression or choice of vocabulary. Suggestions might also be made in relation to the cohesion of the piece and sequencing of ideas. At the proofreading stage the response partner might focus on the presentational aspects including spelling and punctuation. Lucy McCormick Calkins (1983) provides some detailed examples of how children were inducted into responding to each other's writing. In her book pp. 129–30, she lists a series of questions which the children found helpful, including:

- What is the most important thing you are saying?
- Which is the most important part of you story? Why?
- Are there places where you could describe more?
- Is there any other way you could order this?

If children are carefully trained as response partners, it can help them reflect on their writing and evaluate it. Partners need to be paired thoughtfully. Friendship and compatibility might be one basis for struggling writers while for the most able children in the class, pairing by ability might provide more challenge and lead to improvements in the revised drafts of children's writing.

WRITING ON THE SCREEN

Over the last few years, the use of computers to support the writing process has become a much more familiar sight in classrooms. Most classes have their own computer(s) and the range of 'easy-use' word processing programmes is steadily increasing and improving. There are practical issues that need to be addressed at the planning, organisational and resourcing level in order to give the computer a central role. The easy part is to turn the computer on and set up a programme. The hard part is to make sure that the computer is used integrally within the children's writing activities and not as an extension activity after other work has been completed. So, the starting point is planning. In the early years we should be planning activities that familiarise the child with the alphabetic nature of the keyboard and young children will need time to explore and play with the computer. 'Talking' programmes are especially useful as they give the child immediate feedback and guidance. (See Chapter 5 for details of some of these packages.) If you have other adults in the class, then plan for them to work with pairs of children composing collaborative pieces of writing directly onto the computer. The fact that multiple copies can be printed ensures that the children have something immediate, that looks good and can be taken home. Further copies can be produced for display and record keeping purposes in the classroom. Programmes such as *Easy Book* (Sunburst for WINPC or Mac, REM) enable children to put their work into the format of a real book. This programme also has a clip art facility and speech support. Another programme that is well suited to younger writers is *Kidworks 2* (Davidson for WINPC or Mac) which helps children to create talking books. *Kids Works Deluxe* (ABLAC on CD for WINPC and Mac) is a programme for all ages which enables children to write, record and animate stories, books and poems. It includes twenty-five story starts.

As they get more experienced, children can use the word processor to enhance the drafting stage of their writing. By being introduced to tools such as 'cut' and 'paste', grammar and spellcheckers and the thesaurus, the child can undertake revising and editing tasks systematically and with less physical effort. Many packages now offer a wide array of fonts, tools and layouts which will support Key Stage Two children in particular who are expected to make decisions about layout and presentation and are also required to produce different finished products such as guidebooks and pamphlets. A talking word processing programme like *Talking Pendown* (Logotron for Acorn) gives children the facility to create newsletters, cards and posters.

The computer can also raise the self-esteem of struggling writers, especially those with handwriting and spelling difficulties. It is not unusual to see children with specific learning difficulties using their own laptops for a wide range of class work and many programmes have been specifically designed with the struggling writer in mind (see examples in Chapter 5 for spelling and Chapter 7). Concept keyboard overlays can be tailored to the needs of children in the earliest stages of learning English as an Additional Language.

Organisationally, children working in pairs seem best suited to the computer and in older classes these could be the pairings that have been set up as 'writing partners'. If access to computers is limited, then it will be necessary to maintain a rota system to ensure that all the children have a fair chance to use the packages. It is important to ensure that both boys and girls receive an equal opportunity to work with computers and it may help to monitor this on the class rota as well. Finally, remember that many children will already be highly computer literate because they have considerable experience of using computers at home. Encourage them to share their expertise and find out about the packages they are using outside school.

...KING

...ing is about the final stage of the writing process: publication. Although it does not receive a direct mention in the current Programmes of Study for writing, its place is acknowledged in the *NLS* (p. 20 and p. 29). Bookmaking sends out powerful signals to children that their writing will have an active future life and a real purpose. If we make books, we assume that we have a readership who will respond to and be interested in our efforts. Books made by children can form part of the class or school library collection and be read aloud at story time. Ideally, children should be encouraged to make their own books, an activity which can easily be linked with Design and Technology. However, time may be of the essence, and for this reason books can be made in varying levels of sophistication from simple folded ones, such as concertina books, to the hardback, fully-bound variety. For practical suggestions consult Paul Johnson's *Children Making Books* (1995).

Some teachers include bookmaking resources within or alongside their writing area. Such resources include:

- variety of staplers (including long arm)
- small size trimmer
- comb binder
- needles, thread, scissors
- paper
- boards for covers
- bookbinding tape
- glue
- offcuts of wrapping paper or wallpaper (for covers)
- instructions and ready-made examples.

There is a financial implication here and bookmaking materials can be expensive to provide. However, the 'Blue Peter' spirit can prevail and alternative materials can be improvised quite easily. If space is limited, then a tray with compartments can be used to store the materials.

PARENTAL INVOLVEMENT

It was research into literacy before schooling such as that of Gordon Wells (1987), Glenda Bissex (1980) and Shirley Brice Heath (1983) which drew attention to the key role of parents in introducing their children to reading and writing. Parents have always helped their children with reading and writing but for many years teachers were either unaware of this or did not actively encourage such involvement. As recently as the 1980s, it was understandable and not uncommon to hear parents saying such things as, 'We don't want to go against school' and showing some wariness about becoming actively involved in their children's reading and writing. However, home-school reading partnerships (or PACT schemes, as some were known) began to flourish at about that time and marked the clearest sign of a shift in attitudes. Schools quickly realised that a two-way dialogue with parents was positively advantageous and supportive to children's development. Some schools took parental involvement another step further by using the 'parent conference' from *The Primary Language*

Record (Barrs *et al.*, 1988) as a method of providing two-way information about the child's development in reading and writing. Another appreciable advance has been the increased role of parents inside school, supporting reading and writing in the classroom. One of the most positive benefits has been that parents and teachers are able to communicate on a much more regular basis and share their expertise and understanding.

Many schools who have children who speak English as an Additional Language have been able to tap into the languages spoken and written at home. Parents have been approached to help with the translation of reading and writing material and to put stories and rhymes onto tape. Where writing is concerned, teachers have sometimes been surprised to discover that children whom they may have perceived to be struggling as writers of English are in fact, writing confidently in their home and community languages. *The Primary Language Record* and Hilary Minns (1990) provide further details on the importance of maintaining the child's first language in the service of learning a second. They also point out the value of teachers having an awareness of the home based literacy experiences of EAL learners.

Parents can be involved at many levels in their child's writing development, both formally and informally. With the youngest children, at an informal level, you can try out a 'Home Writing' board or 'Our Messages' board in the classroom which can encourage children to bring in pieces of writing they have done at home. Such pieces will come in all shapes or forms. They might be handwriting practice on the back of an envelope, a list of family names on a scrap of paper or a computer written story. In one class, a child brought in a copy of the alphabet written in Arabic script. Another brought in a story that he had written, which his parents had translated into Spanish. The resulting excitement and pleasure that the sharing of this writing has for both pupils and teachers indicates that it is a very positive and worthwhile activity to encourage.

At a more formal level, schools will have a whole-school policy on the involvement of parents and the level of commitment expected on each side. Some schools have established formal contracts with their parents in order to guarantee support for children's reading and writing development at home. It is not uncommon now to see short booklets or brochures which are given to parents, explaining the school's approach to reading and writing. These booklets may give detailed information about the ways in which handwriting and spelling are to be taught. In addition, information might also be provided about the school's marking policy for writing so that parents are not dismayed or puzzled by the teachers' response to the children's use of invented spellings. In Key Stage Two, parents may also be asked to participate in the school's homework policy which is likely to include the regular learning of spellings and writing assignments to be completed at home and brought into school. Relationships with parents are particularly important when you are dealing with children with learning difficulties.

SELF-HELP STRATEGIES

It will have become clear in this chapter that writing routines are underpinned by a careful balance of direct teaching and independent activity. Through direct teaching, we take responsibility, and can model explicitly to the children how the routine works and why it is useful to us as writers. In their independent writing, children can try the routines out for themselves. Our observations of children while engaged in the routines will inform us of areas of strength and elements that require further teaching from us (see Chapter 6). In the Literacy Hour, the ability to utilise self-help strategies is crucially important during the period when the teacher is targeting two groups each day for guided reading or guided writing. The groups engaged in independent work need a wide range of strategies to enable them to maintain their independence and avoid disturbing the groups working with the teacher.

These strategies for independence are not learnt overnight. They will require repeated demonstrations from the teacher, especially in the early stages. McCormick Calkins (1983) describes these as 'mini-lessons'. In the early days with a new class, monitor carefully what makes the different routines operate smoothly. Identify strategies which promote independence within each routine and explain these to the children. Check how successfully the children cope with the self-help strategies that you give to them and make amendments as necessary. Try to avoid continuing to ask children to work with a strategy that is not effective. One of the best ways to work on self-help strategies is to involve the children themselves by discussing the problem with them and asking them to offer solutions. One class solved their spelling queue problem by devising their own list of strategies for finding a spelling. Their list was placed as a reminder poster on the wall. By involving the children, we are helping them to reflect on the problem for themselves and encouraging them to take control of possible ways of managing it. (See also Chapter 5 under Independence and risk taking.)

In this final section of the chapter are some questions to ask yourself when preparing to promote self-help strategies in the classroom.

Resources

Have I:

- made necessary resources permanently available?
- got fixed places for permanently available resources?
- made available everything that the children need for specific activities?
- got enough resources to go around the groups?
- ensured that the resources are within reach?
- told the children where to find the resources they need?

Ground rules for using resources

Have I made clear to the children:

- what they can/cannot help themselves to?
- the use and care of shared resources e.g. rubbers and sharpeners?
- that some items can only be used by a limited number of people at any one time e.g. computer?
- that they should only take what they need?
- that some scarce resources can only be used for limited periods of time when they are actually needed within an activity?

- that they should handle expensive resources carefully?
- that anything that is borrowed must be returned to its place at the earliest possible time?
- what to do with left-over resources that need tidying up?

Writing resources which require careful organisation

The computer

Have I:

- set the computer up each day with the appropriate programme?
- carried out a daily maintenance check e.g. paper in printer?
- instructed all the children on basic operating instructions?
- instructed all the children on basic troubleshooting strategies?
- provided a set of simple operating instructions and troubleshooting cards (with diagrams and icons) near the computer?
- made the children aware of items on computer that can help with different aspects of writing e.g. spellchecker?
- clarified when these items should/should not be used e.g. cut and paste for drafting?
- established a rota for usage?

Dictionaries, word banks and word books

Have I:

- checked that a suitable range is available?
- taught the children in shared sessions how to access dictionaries?
- created word banks of words in current high usage e.g. key words for class topic (illustrated if necessary)?
- made alphabet strips available to help locate the position of letters in dictionaries?
- set ground rules for the use of personal word books?
- drawn up a reminder poster on how to succeed in finding a word?
- promoted independent spelling strategies?
- taught the use of the thesaurus and encouraged children to use it?

Self-help strategies and the individual child

Getting started

Have I:

- carefully explained the process and purpose of the writing routine to be practised?
- drawn attention to self-help strategies that may come in useful?
- taught or re-taught specific self-help strategies?
- made a set of attractive and briefly worded 'reminder' cards of key points (colour coded depending on aspect of writing process e.g. pink for spelling, yellow for punctuation etc.)?

Getting stuck

Have I:

- demonstrated to the class what I do when I'm stuck with my writing?
- agreed with the child that self-help strategies must be tried first?
- encouraged the child to have a go at solving his/her problem using his/her own ideas and initiative?
- encouraged peer group support at solving problems?
- encouraged the child to move on to next part of task which s/he can do independently and then go back to the problem area?

If all else fails

Have I:

- told the child which relevant, alternative 'holding' activities can be carried out?
- agreed a last resort system of making contact with me if help is absolutely essential?

Good luck!

FURTHER READING

CLPE (1990) *Shared Reading Shared Writing*. London: CLPE.

Czerniewska, P. (1992) 'Becoming a Writer', in *Learning about Writing*. Oxford: Blackwell.

Gregory, A. *et al.* (1991) *Writers' Workshop*. Stoke on Trent: Trentham Books.

Hall, N. and Robinson, A. (1995) *Exploring Writing and Play in the Early Years*. London: David Fulton Publishers.

Merttens, R. *et al.* (1996) 'Parental Involvement in Writing', in *Learning in Tandem Involving Parents in their Children's Education*, Chapter 4. Leamington Spa: Scholastic.

Smith, J. and Elley, W. (1997) 'Technologies and Writing', in *How Children Learn to Write*, Chapter 4. London: Paul Chapman.

CHAPTER 4

Composition

Fiona M. Collins

COMPOSITION AND RANGE

> Composition is what powers the writing. It is vital that the focus, in relation to children's writing, is first and foremost on composition, and that children perceive that this is so.
> (Barrs, 1987; p. 2)

What is composition?

Composition is about creating ideas, developing individual voice and being able to write in different forms for a range of purposes and audiences. This chapter looks at what we understand by composition, its place in the writing process and how children can be encouraged to extend and develop their range of writing in both narrative and non-narrative genres.

As we saw in Chapter 2, there is a useful distinction to be made between 'composition' and 'transcription' in the writing process. Smith shows it in this way:

Composition	*Transcription*
(author)	(secretary)
getting ideas	physical effort of writing
selecting words	spelling
grammar	capitalisation
	punctuation
	paragraphs
	legibility

(1982, p. 20)

Composition, like any imaginative or creative process, involves a willingness to take risks and impose order on one's thoughts. It is important that children do not feel constrained when writing by difficulties in controlling the secretarial aspects; as Barrs says 'the focus . . . is first and foremost on composition.'

The National Curriculum Programmes of Study for writing recognise this distinction and cover composition and transcription, which they call 'presentation'. The three sub-headings which are used throughout the *National Curriculum* (Range, Key Skills, Standard English and Language Study) will be referred to in this chapter though some aspects of Key Skills belong to Chapter 5. Within Range at Key Stages One and Two the following areas are covered: organising and developing ideas; writing in response to stimuli; identifying a purpose for their writing; writing for a range of readers; organising and presenting ideas in different ways; and writing in a range of forms.

The *NLS* covers this range, and adds that:

Literate primary pupils should:

- know, understand and be able to write in a range of genres in fiction and poetry, and understand and be familiar with some of the ways in which narratives are structured through basic literary ideas of setting, character and plot;
- understand, use and be able to write a range of non-fiction texts;
- through reading and writing, develop their powers of imagination, inventiveness and critical awareness.

(1998, p. 3)

Writing is explicitly taught within the framework of English, whether it is in Literacy Hours or in other English sessions. However children are also asked to write in other curriculum areas, such as history, geography or science. Thus progress and development can be fostered and monitored in writing across the curriculum.

Audience, purpose and context

Audience, purpose and context help the young writer to develop a voice and gradually control the written word to make meaning.

Children often write with a particular audience in mind such as other members of the class, younger children, their parents, the local community or an organisation. These audiences may be known or unknown. For young children, it is important that audience is identified from the outset because it helps with decisions about tone, choice of language and structure. The *National Curriculum* requires that Key Stage One children write for 'their teacher, their family, their peers and themselves' and at Key Stage Two this range widens to include 'adults in the school and community and imagined audiences'. The *NLS* gives detailed and specific suggestions for children to vary 'appropriateness of style, vocabulary and presentation' according to audience. Sometimes such real and varied audiences are difficult to contrive, and role-play, discussed later, can be used as a context to provide imaginary audiences.

The purpose of the writing also affects composition, whether it be to entertain, persuade or explain. Purpose influences the linguistic structure of the piece and helps the child consider the language choices to be made. The purpose of the writing also links with the form that the writing will take; maybe a letter, diary or pamphlet. It should not be forgotten that one form of writing can be used for different purposes and different audiences; just think of all the different pamphlets you see in a week.

The context for the writing provides purpose and gives the writer direction and involvement in the piece; a purposeful context can also be motivating and encouraging. Writing arising from a class story or poem can stimulate children to write imaginatively, in the role of authors creating imaginary worlds and characters. As you saw in Chapter 3, the provision of role-play contexts for writing is most important for children.

As well as teacher provided contexts, children are often motivated to write from their own interests, reading and life experiences. Television and video stories, characters and events are important influences and frequently appear in children's writing, sometimes in the same story as favourite book characters. Such influences can affect the plot of the story, pace, style and the use of dialogue. The influence of popular culture is often short-lived as one fashion replaces another. However, although the particular programme may disappear, the impact of popular culture on children's writing will always be apparent.

The links between reading and writing are strong and widely recognised. The more children read, the more their work reflects wider horizons, the more they employ book language to create feelings, thoughts and questions, the more they experiment with plots, themes, ideas. The *NLS* acknowledges this: 'Writing is closely linked to reading – the two activities reinforce each other. . . . The context of pupils' reading, i.e. the texts, gives structures, themes and purposes for much of their writing' (DfEE, 1998, p. 5).

First-hand experiences and interests colour much children's writing and indeed are at the heart of all talented composition. Many small boys will turn all their stories into football accounts as you can see in this five year old's story:

> A Match at Wembley
> Once there were eleven tigers and eleven lions. All the lions and tigers fans came to Wembley stadium. They were going to play a football match. Everyone in the whole nation came to watch. . . .

It is however sometimes difficult to persuade older children that their experiences merit written exploration and attention but writing about what you know intimately nearly always results in better writing.

In this discussion on audience, purpose and context, we should remember that writing is not always in the public domain. It is also for thinking and learning. It is important that children are encouraged to write down their feelings or to use writing to reflect on what they have actually learnt, for instance, in a science lesson. Myra Barrs argues that activities that link writing and learning are just as important as those driven by audience and purpose and she quotes Katherine Perera: 'Writing is not merely a way of recording speech, but a different form of language in its own right which can lead to different forms of thinking' (1991, p. 1).

Categorising writing

Writing can be divided into two broad categories: narrative and non-narrative (or fiction and non-fiction). Although these are loose categories and there is some overlap, they are helpful as the separate characteristics of each can be identified and deliberately used by new writers.

The characteristics of narrative writing are: characters, settings, problems, solutions and resolutions. Narratives may be set in the present, in another time, in this country or another place. They may be realistic or fantastic. The main purpose of narrative writing is to entertain the reader. In children's literature, there are many different types of narrative writing such as traditional tales, adventure stories, historical stories and personal narratives. As far as children's writing is concerned, the *National Curriculum* does not specify the types of narrative but expects children to write in 'a range of forms, incorporating some of the different characteristics of those forms' (p. 9). The *NLS* requires children to write from personal experience, to compose myths, fables, traditional tales (typically predictable and patterned), playscripts and poems (which will not always be narratives). By Year 6, the children are expected to be reading and writing, at least in modest ways, such narratives as mystery, humour, sci-fi, historical and fantasy. The requirement to parody a literary text (Year 6.2) clearly depends on secure identification of narrative features.

Non-narrative writing, unlike narrative writing, is not just to entertain (although it often does) but is written for different purposes and for different audiences. It is not about specific characters and their problems but is about general matters, processes, arguments. It aims to inform, persuade and instruct. These different purposes and aims give rise to the many different text types, or 'genres', that are characteristic of non-narrative writing. You will remember from Chapter 2 that genres are socially recognised text types, or 'different kinds of writing that have different functions in written discourse and in society' (Barrs, 1991; p. 9). The genre of a piece of writing influences the overall structure of the text and language choices made within the piece of writing. The work of Maureen Lewis and David Wray (1995) for the EXEL project was established to look at ways of improving children's writing in different genres. They identified six non-fiction genres used regularly within our society (recount, report, procedural, explanation, persuasion and discussion) and they argue that children need to understand the structural and linguistic differences between the genres.

Katherine Perera (1984), among others, classifies writing in a rather different way. Rather than using narrative and non-narrative she employs the terms 'chronological' or 'non-chronological'. In other words, writing can either be structured and organised with reference to time, or not. The *NLS* bases its definitions of chronological and non-chronological writing on Perera, defining them as 'writing organised in terms of sequences of events' (*NLS*, p. 75) or 'writing organised without reference to time sequence' (*NLS*, p. 83). Examples of chronological writing are: directions to a particular place; a recount of a day visit; a recipe or a mystery story. You will see that this list includes both narrative and non-narrative writing. All of this is not intended to confuse; the fact is that chronological writing, narrative or non-narrative, is easier for young writers to manage than non-chronological writing and so there are implications for your teaching. For those of you working with older children you will need to pay careful attention to the planning of non-chronological writing which becomes more of a challenge once you lose time and sequence as an organiser. You will see this if you consider the organisation of these examples of non-chronological writing: reports written in science or geography, a discussion about hunting, or an argument for the banning of whale killing in the world.

Within the *National Curriculum* different forms of writing are prescribed for each Key Stage. At Key Stage One both the form and the genre are linked together, while at Key Stage Two they are separate and defined. So at Key Stage One we find narratives, stories, notes, observations, messages etc. are listed and at Key Stage Two requirements are that children should be 'taught to use the characteristics of different kinds of writing'. Argument, commentary, narrative and dialogue are listed, as is a range of writing forms including: stories, poems, dialogues, drama scripts, non-fiction, reports, instructions, explanations, notes and letters.

Such a range is also identified within the *NLS* which identifies fiction and non-fiction writing with the two strongly linked to reading. The *NLS* range is more specific than in the *National Curriculum* and follows a progressive pattern with form and genre linked at Key Stage One (e.g. signs, labels, instructions). By the end of Key Stage Two specific genres are identified, e.g. persuasive writing, non-chronological reports.

All children are entitled to learn about this range of writing. Recent research, however, confirms that boys are more interested in writing non-narrative than narrative. Thus, if the diet of writing is more weighted towards narrative, boys may become disaffected and disadvantaged. 'If this is an area of the curriculum towards which boys are inclined, then a lack of attention to non-fiction writing may disadvantage them more' (QCA, 1998). See Chapter 7 for more discussion on gender issues in writing.

Biliterate children

Some children are able to compose in different languages and, as you will remember from Chapter 2, this biliteracy is cognitively healthy and needs to be actively encouraged. Composing involves thinking and if you are thinking in one language and being asked to write in another it may not be very easy to be fluent. If this is recognised by the teacher, opportunities can be provided to discuss, plan and compose in first languages, in the early stages of writing. At a later stage the move can be made into English. You may find that children are more comfortable writing straightaway in English when the writing is in school curriculum areas (science, geography etc.) whereas stories, which may spring from early experience in the mother tongue, may be more readily composed in that first language. At an early age some children will experiment with both languages together and there may be evidence of such code-switching in their writing. (See Figure 5.3 later in the book for an example of this.)

Where linguistic diversity is valued and the children's use of different languages and dialects is actively promoted, there are exciting possibilities for joint composition. Two nine year old girls worked intently together to produce a dual-language text in English and Turkish. What you will notice in Figure 4.1 is their delight in offering this 'new' translated version which lures the reader in with the promise of 'jokes all the way along'.

Figure 4.1

NARRATIVE WRITING

Stories have a basic structure: a beginning, a middle and an end. Children quickly realise this from hearing stories read and reading themselves. They also learn about this basic narrative structure from watching cartoons and dramas on children's television. Narratologists have analysed the structures of stories in order to show common patterns or story grammars and such descriptions can help our work with children. For instance Hoey (1983) gives us the following labels which could be easily understood and used by children: 'Situation', 'Problem', 'Solution' and 'Evaluation' (by which Hoey means how everything turns out and what has been learned).

At Key Stage One children may write stories that include familiar characters, settings similar to where they live, and personal experiences. They may also write about characters taken from fiction, exotic settings and fantasy experiences. Such stories may be simply structured with a beginning, perhaps taken from a traditional story ('Once upon a time . . .'), an event, and an ending with a resolution ('. . . and we all went home for tea'). The *NLS*, in acknowledgement of this, has placed emphasis on teaching different aspects of story writing which build on children's natural interest in narrative and books. The Framework states that pupils should be taught 'to write about events in personal experience linked to a variety of familiar incidents from stories' (Year1.1) and 'to use story settings from reading, e.g. redescribe, use in own writing, write a different story in the same setting' (Year 2.2). The question of how children develop their narrative writing is complex. Some young children's narratives will display surprising complexities of plot with narrative twists, chained episodes and the introduction of minor characters. (This is especially true when they are given the opportunity to dictate their stories, see Chapter 3.) This ability to handle complexity may have been acquired through wide reading rather than through being explicitly taught within the primary classroom. However, we cannnot depend on this. As some children get older, they may experience problems with narrative writing such as: poor structure, lack of focus, too many linked incidents, poor endings or unwarranted shifts in narrative voice. The *NLS* suggests explicit teaching at Key Stage Two of the component parts of narrative writing including character descriptions, narrative view point and story structure.

Teaching narrative writing at Key Stage One

This section provides a case study on fable writing carried out with a Year 1 class.

In planning this scheme of work the teacher had to think about the particular features of a fable, how to help children understand the structure of a fable and how to give them support in writing a fable for themselves. She started by reading a selection of Aesop's fables (including *The Fox and the Grapes*, *The Frog and the Stork*, and *The Boy who Cried Wolf*) and she discussed the differences and similarities between them.

The following sequence of activities was intended to encourage the children to think about narrative structure, choice of language and how the plot is linked to the moral. She wanted the children to see that each of the fables has a moral, a structure in common, and uses animal characters.

After the initial readings children retold a fable to one another, showing how important oral storytelling can be for such work as it brings about real personal engagement with the story. (It is particularly appropriate for stories like these which have been told for generations by word of mouth.) After this, the children carried out two written activities: a cloze procedure where they had to replace certain words in the story thus focussing their attention on the meanings of words in context, and a storyboard activity to help them reflect on the sequence of main events in a fable.

The children were then asked to write their own fable using animal characters and including a moral. Before the actual writing started the children brainstormed relevant opening lines such as: 'In a far away land . . .', 'There was once . . .' and 'Long, long ago . . .'. After this the children discussed how such stories could end and two possibilities were decided on: either the characters learn a lesson or they meet a sticky end.

Finally, the teacher wanted to extend the children's use of vocabulary so she discussed descriptive words that the children might use in their writing. Together they compiled a list of useful adjectives which might suit the different characters ('curious', 'greedy', 'vain', 'massive', etc.). These were written on the board as a reference point for the children.

To help their thinking about structure the children were given a storyboard planner on which to plot the basic events of their fable. Michael's completed planner is shown in Figure 4.2.

Figure 4.2

After the planners were completed, the children discussed them with the teacher allowing her to respond to their attempts. This discussion is all-important, as it provides a context for the children to develop their thinking and creativity and also to be shown any problems in their story structure. Then, with their planners beside them, the children started their own independent story writing. The teacher continued to discuss their writing with them and enabled the kind of development below by Rebecca. This is the first draft of her writing:

> The Cow and the Mirror
> Once upon a time in a far away land lived a cow. The cow was very vain. The cow kept looking at herself in the mirror. One day the mirror smashed.

At this point Rebecca thought she had finished, but after discussion with the teacher she continued:

> . . . into tiny pieces. She found a river and she went closer and saw her reflection. She got so close that she fell in the water. She was very sorry for herself and learned her lesson not to be so vain.

The completed story is more sophisticated in structure, with the moral linking quite clearly with the events of the story.

Finally, here is Michael's completed fable:

> The Tiger and the Zebra
> In a hot country called Africa there lived a bright orange tiger who was so proud of his stripes. The tiger really couldn't think of another animal that had them. Every day he went to show off to the other animals. Then he went to sleep feeling very very proud of himself. When he woke up and went to show off to the other animals he saw a zebra and that zebra had stripes just like him. He was very upset with himself. He was so upset he couldn't sleep or speak to other animals because he was so upset. The moral of the story is don't show off.

In this we see Michael's grasp of story 'grammar'. He provides an opening 'situation', a tiger living in Africa. The 'problem' is that the tiger believes he is the only animal with stripes and thus becomes very vain; the 'solution' is that he sees the zebra and realises other animals have stripes; and the 'evaluation' is that he learns a lesson which is not to show off. Such well organised, lively and coherent writing is a direct result of the teacher's well thought through approach to the teaching of narrative structure in fables.

Traditional stories are not, of course, the only narratives to be worked on at Key Stage One. Children will want to write in many other ways and it is important to support and respond to their interests and efforts.

Teaching narrative writing at Key Stage Two

In this section, the teaching of more complex narrative aspects such as characterisation, more varied beginnings and endings, settings and descriptions, and narrator's point of view are considered.

Characterisation

At Key Stage Two the *NLS* requires work on characters stating that pupils should be taught to, 'write character sketches, focusing on small details to evoke sympathy or dislike' (Year 4.1). For children to develop characters in stories, they need to consider the techniques writers use to depict character. An obvious technique is to give character details through the narrator's description of what the character looks like, their past, their thoughts and their actions. A second device is to allow characters to reveal themselves through direct speech. An author can also show us the character through the thoughts of other people in the story. To draw on all these techniques it is useful to give children a checklist of questions:

- What does the character look like?
- What do other people think of them?
- What are the typical things this character would say?
- What are they seen doing?

The most common of these techniques – narrative description – is explored below and concludes with a piece of writing by a Year 6 girl, Rachel, which demonstrates all the above techniques in her competent characterisation.

Young writers need to be reassured that they can draw from the people they know, their friends and family, as well as people they read about. Many teachers ask children to compose descriptions for their classmates to identify. They can be reminded of memorable characters they have met in their own reading (Tom from *Tom's Midnight Garden* or maybe Dahl's Big Friendly Giant) and help them to see how the author uses the above techniques. Consider a passage such as this initial paragraph from a short story by Bill Naughton where he introduces us, through a narrator's description, to the main character:

> Spit Nolan was a pal of mine. He was a thin lad with a bony face that was always pale, except for rosy spots on his cheekbones. He had quick brown eyes, rather stooped shoulders, and we all knew that he had only one lung. He had had a disease which in those days couldn't be cured, unless you went away to Switzerland, which Spit certainly couldn't afford. He wasn't sorry for himself in any way, and in fact we envied him, because he never had to go to school. (1970, p. 20)

Using such a passage, you might ask the children to highlight the things they learn about Spit in one short paragraph: his appearance, his disability, his poverty and his positive outlook. From this activity, the children could then carry out a 'search' for similar objective descriptions in their reading.

To conclude this section, here is the beginning of the third chapter of Rachel's World War Two saga:

> Father At War
> A few days after the scene in the dining room there were hasty goodbyes at the railway station, my mother talked on about eating well and not getting to sleep too late until my father gave her a brief hug, a quick peck on the cheek and disappeared into the crowds of uniformed men.
> 'Well that's your father off,' she said briskly to us and tickled me on the tummy, I stared back at her with big eyes.
> 'Well come on' she snapped as if cross at me for not laughing as my tummy was very ticklish. When we got home mother busied herself in the kitchen making tea. Mary, George and I scrambled up the stairs and into Mary's room where we all sat on the bed and talked. We talked about the war and all the changes that would come into our lives. We talked about father and what he would be doing now. Mary was scared and she and I cried, me clinging onto Mary like a rag doll.
> George was brave and stern now that he was the man of the house but I often saw a flicker of fear pass through his eyes.'

In shared text work, the teacher could show the class how Rachel has portrayed the mother's character through narrator's description ('she snapped'); through an account of actions (she 'tickled me', she 'busied herself in kitchen'); through direct speech ("Well, that's your father off!") and through other characters' thoughts (she 'talked on about eating well'). The class could then go on to look at how she has characterised Mary, George and the narrator.

Tantalising beginnings and satisfying endings

A good beginning will engage readers and encourage them to want to read on. They will want to go on to discover the story, answer questions that have been posed and to fill gaps that have been left by the author. Many an author hints at secrets that will be revealed later in the book (as in the opening of *Gulf* in the example below). Reading a range of literature allows children to experience different beginnings and consider the ways that authors engage the reader's attention. Some use arresting dialogue: '"Where's Papa going with that axe?" said Fern' from *Charlotte's Web* (E. B. White); some involve us immediately with the character's dilemmas: 'I loved my brother. Right from the start. But did I love him enough? You shouldn't use people you love. Maybe what happened to him was all my fault. . . .' *Gulf* (Robert Westall); and some shock us with the drama of the opening statement: 'When Bill Simpson woke up on Monday morning, he found he was a girl' *Bill's New Frock* (Anne Fine).

As children develop their reading and writing so their personal beginnings start to diversify. Below is a selection of Key Stage Two beginnings that mirror the different categories discussed above:

And what do you think you are doing in my garden? snapped Mary.
(Year 6)

Suddenly everything went dark, I panicked.
(Year 5)

It was on a Sunday evening when I went to church to say my prayers, when all of a sudden a beam of light shone down on me.
(Year 6)

However it is not only the first few lines that make an impact on the reader; it is also the first page. Comparing interesting and dull first pages will help children think about their own writing. Try looking at the first page of a book like *Cold Shoulder Road* (Joan Aiken). What is it that makes us want to read on?

Every night, around nine o'clock in Cold Shoulder Road, the screaming began. It came from the end house in the row. It was not very loud. The sound was like the cries of the gulls who flew and whirled along the shingle-bank on the seaward side of the road.
People who lived in the road (there were not many of them) took no notice of the screaming. It's the gull, they thought, or the wind: or, whatever it is, it's no business of ours.
Only one person felt differently, and she lived next door to the house from which the screaming came.
Night after night she clenched her hands and stood trembling by the window.
Something has got to be done, she thought. Something must be done.
At last she did it.

The impact of repeated words ('gull', 'screaming'), short paragraphs and the closing focus on the girl with her clenched hands who is going to take action all contribute to the power and tension of this opening.

Completing a story may be difficult for the young writer, especially if the organisation of the story does not support a conclusion. Often children's stories conclude weakly with 'I woke up and it was all a dream' or 'I went home to have my tea'. To move children on from this stage it is important to discuss endings of favourite novels with the class, to find out if they were satisfying and left a feeling of 'Yes, I agree with this'. As with beginnings, different endings do different things: some answer questions, some leave questions unanswered and some raise new questions. Endings can entail physical movement, for instance a person walking out of sight along a road, a character travelling to a new country or getting into a car and looking back. All these leave the reader with the impression that the story is moving on, and that the narrative continues even though the book has finished. These and other techniques discussed here leave the reader with a sense of fulfilment in the narrative and it is worth spending time with children looking at interesting endings such as this one in Michael Rosen's *The Bakerloo Flea*:

> She told me I was the first person she'd ever told the story to, and told me never to tell anyone. The scandal would be terrible. I don't know whether to believe her or not.

Such work will help children reflect on their own writing, just as Ricky (Year 5) did: 'It was a really exciting story. Only I knew who the burglar was till the end when I revealed ALL – like on the telly!'

The key to a good ending lies in the planning and structure of the story, although this will not always come when you start the planning. Once the writer has established the basic structure of the plot and started writing then the ending or resolution will fit more easily into place. Planning is discussed later in this chapter.

To end with a satisfying ending, here is Rachel's (Year 6) 'epilogue' to her World War Two family saga, *Father at War* (see p. 51):

> I never saw Mrs Whitby again, but I will never forget her. Some memories cannot be forgotten. Like the war, not that a war is an easy thing to forget, with all its deaths, bombs, battles. I want to forget the war, like waking up from a bad dream, but as much as I try I know I will never forget it.

Point of view

A story can be written in the first or third person although most narrative writing for children is in the third person. Narrators may, in 'omniscient' mode, tell us everything a character or characters are doing, thinking and feeling. Alternatively, narrators may only 'report' on their characters' actions and leave readers to infer how they must feel and think. Just as in first person narratives, a single character is usually the focus of the narrator's attention. We as readers usually have no problem in knowing who is the character to watch. Writing in the first person is something children will be doing readily in their recounts: 'We were in Lanzarote and we went to the lagoon. I said to my Mum "Can't I go scuba diving with Emma my new friend I met at the swings?"' (Year 4). However, making the kind of shift to first person narrative writing that Rachel, in the above examples, does so successfully usually requires teacher support. Children need to understand that the first person narrator does not have to be them, but may be a fictitious person telling the story from his or her point of view, as the wolf does in *The True Story of the Three Little Pigs* (Jon Scieszka):

> Everyone knows the story of the Three little Pigs. Or at least they think they do. But I'll let you into a little secret. Nobody knows the real story, because nobody has ever heard *my* side of the story.

Considering another person's perspective can be difficult but placing children in imaginary situations allows them to write successfully as a particular character, as this Year 5 writer has done taking the role of the dormouse in her revisiting of the Mad Hatter's tea-party:

> The Mad Hatter and the March Hare were having their tea. I was asleep. Alice had just sat down after the Mad Hatter had said, 'No room!'. Alice started telling us her story when all of a sudden she brought Dina into it. Dina is her cat!
>
> 'Cat!' I yelled. I jumped up and ran into the Mad Hatter's arms. The Mad Hatter asked the March Hare to give him some treacle to put on my nose. I love treacle. After that I was put back in the teapot and I went back to sleep.

Planning and structuring plots

As well as engaging the reader's attention at the beginning of the story, the writer needs to build up the plot and 'focus on language to create effects, e.g. building tension, suspense, creating moods, setting scenes' (*NLS*). As we saw with the fable example, thoughtful planning helps children to be creative and imaginative within a scaffolded approach.

A young writer needs time to think and create as story writing seldom happens instantaneously. Ideally, time should be taken to think about and internalise the task. Some children will draw during this time, others will discuss their ideas with their writing partners (see Chapter 3), and others will search for inspiration in earlier pieces of writing and in books. Preliminary work on characters and setting could be done during the Literacy Hour while the extended writing itself could be done outside this period when the children have the time needed to work on longer pieces.

Story planners or prompts help structure narrative, as well as prompting ideas. Some children will need more structure than others and it is advisable to differentiate according to need. Below is an example of some planning prompts which can be adjusted to meet the different needs. These could be organised in clearly delineated sections.

> Story planner
> Who are you writing the story for (audience)?
> What is the story about (plot)?
> What type of story is it (adventure, horror, fantasy, historical or other)?
> Who are the main characters?
> Where and when is the story set?
> Who is telling the story and how much do they know (narrator's voice)?
> What is the first sentence? Have you interested the reader?
> Ideas for the ending? (These can be added to as you are writing the story.)

Alongside planning, an important aspect of any young writer's work is the continuing discussion and feedback which usefully take place during the process of writing. Even when the work is complete, sharing with an audience will also give children opportunities to sharpen and improve their writing.

Narrative writing engages children's imaginations. It allows them to explore the literary world for themselves and become real authors. In order to do this children need careful support and structure offered through interactions with books and teachers.

Further reading

Graves, D. (1989) *Experiment with Fiction*. Portsmouth, New Hampshire: Heinemann.

Thomas, H. (1998) 'Working with Story Structure', in *Reading and Responding to Fiction: Classroom Strategies for Developing Literature*, Chapter 1. Leamington Spa: Scholastic.

Wyse, D. (1998) 'The Development of Composition', in *Primary Writing*, Chapter 3. Buckingham: Open University Press.

POETRY WRITING

> Reading and writing poetry helps me understand myself, clarify my thoughts and see things in a new way. It keeps the mind alert and also satisfies that basic urge we have to create something unique.
> (Brownjohn, 1994; p. 15)

Young children demonstrate an early interest in playing with rhyme and rhythm. Songs, advertisements, TV jingles, nursery rhymes, rhyming stories, finger and action rhymes foster and exploit this early delight in language. As they get older they find that poetry comes in different forms, not always rhyming, and is to be found on the page as well as in the ear. They learn that words in poetry have been memorably ordered to represent feeling. They learn that Walter de la Mare can evoke moonlight perfectly, just as Michael Rosen can sum up how they feel about a younger sibling.

Children will find out about these joys when enthusiastic adults surround them with the work of many poets. We need to read a great deal to them and let the poems and poets do the work for us. We can be sure that poets like John Agard, Charles Causley and Christina Rossetti will work their magic! Sandy Brownjohn reminds us that 'The teacher should be interested in and enthusiastic about poetry; otherwise the children themselves will be indifferent towards it' (1980, p. 85). Many schools have found that a visit from a poet who shares his or her working approaches results in increased confidence and interest in writing poetry. By sharing and enjoying poetry children will realise that they too can represent images and feelings through words which they choose and work on with care. Six year old Claire did just that with her first poem:

> Out in the playground
> Mark stands at the top of the slide
> Afraid to come down.

In the above example, Claire has not only worked from her own observations and understanding of feeling, but she has also benefited from her teacher's help in looking at form, in this case the three line haiku. Such inspection of form is an important part of teaching children to compose poetry. The *NLS* states that Reception children should build on their knowledge of poetry by 'retelling, substitution, extension, and . . . shared composition with adults.' In Years 1 and 2, the *NLS* suggests that such work should be extended through language play, through inventing their 'own riddles, language puzzles, jokes, nonsense sentences etc., derived from reading; . . . tongue twisters or alliterative sentences' (p. 30). Sandy Brownjohn states: 'I separate all the individual details which go to make the whole. Every part is understood as it is conquered' (1994, p. 7). Brownjohn advocates that teaching different techniques to children will develop their skills as composers of poetry, encourage them to play with language, give them the freedom to manipulate words and allow them to control what they say. She suggests that a great deal of this type of work can be carried out through games and puzzles. Her 'The Furniture Game' (1994, p. 19) helps children with description and develops their use of metaphor and simile. It is a guessing game with one child thinking of a person that the rest of the children know and describing this person as a piece of furniture, a plant, a type of food and a time of day. The following example comes from a Year 4 child. Look at the way in which the exercise has enabled her to follow her three similes with a metaphor:

> She is like a cushion
> She is like a sweet smelling rose
> She is like a cheesy pizza
> This person is an afternoon person.

This child and her classmates were being encouraged to appreciate the effects you can create through manipulating language. Just four lines of this sort of work can be put on the page and can start to look like a poem.

At this stage children need to know that there are formal ways of crafting poetry and they will enjoy experimenting with these. In the *NLS* there is comprehensive coverage of the forms that can be shared and taught across the primary age range. Some are specified for introducing to younger children (playground chants, tongue twisters) and others are for older children (e.g. limericks, riddles). The teacher can model these different forms in shared writing. However, it may be helpful to understand that many poetic forms can be regarded as frameworks which children will use at any age if they know about them, to help shape their writing. The success with which they do this will be determined by maturity, experience and ability, and obviously by the appropriateness of the form; if you want to lament your cat's death you are more likely to choose the form of an elegy rather than a limerick.

One such form that all poets enjoy is shape (or concrete) poetry, where the poem is written in the shape of the object that is being written about. A very young child might enjoy making a shape poem to represent a snail. George Herbert, the seventeenth century poet, made a sophisticated shape poem in the shape of angel's wings. Figure 4.3 is written by a Year 4 child in the shape of a rose.

As well as being given support with technique and form, children need to be aware that poetry springs from many different starting points but particularly from 'personal or imagined experience' (*NLS*, p. 39). Michael Rosen, a poet who has inspired so many children in recent decades, believes that better poetry is written if children value their

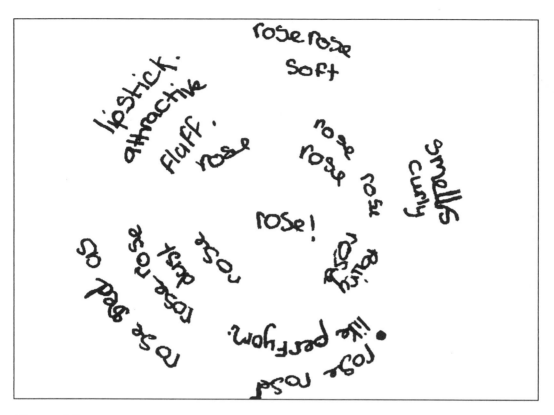

Figure 4.3

own experiences ('I broke my mum's vase yesterday'), using the actual words that people speak ('That's my favourite vase you've broken') and their own responses and feelings ('Why does she keep going on at me? She shouldn't have left it in the sink anyway.') All of this can be the stuff of their poetry. 'My point in asking children to write down what people say and what they think, is that this is knowledge they already possess. It isn't something they have to concoct or translate' (1989, p. 43). Jill Pirrie (1987), a teacher who has inspired so many children, believes that the close observation that she encourages in her children, whether it be of ants in the grass outside the school or of how they feel about a promise being broken, is what lies behind an effective poem.

Such work can be particularly empowering for children who are regarded as 'low achievers'. If these children work with familiar content, with a prescribed and supportive framework, and with no expectation that they have to write at length, then they have a real opportunity to compose successfully in ways that they may not be able to do in prose. As Sandy Brownjohn states:

> Teachers should be prepared to be surprised by the good quality of writing that may soon be in evidence from children who were hitherto low achievers. In fact, it is not always the most able children who write the best poetry in schools.
> (1994, p. 5)

In the writing of poetry the points that are made throughout this book about process (issues such as drafting) and product (issues such as presentation and publishing) are particularly significant. When children are working on what are often quite short stretches of text, then the motivation to shape and work on writing is enhanced. Children's poetry should not only be published, decorated and displayed but also performed to other children and parents. Many teachers make anthologies and tape collections of children's poetry which are highly motivating. All of this will contribute to the sense of audience and purpose with which they can approach the composing.

Teaching poetry writing involves experiencing poems, exploring words and language, looking at different forms and believing in the validity of one's own experience. 'The pursuit of form, coupled with the encouragement to revise and refine first impressions, leads writers back to their experiences and makes them respond more deeply to them'. (Tunnicliffe, 1984; p. 151).

Finally, Figure 4.4 is a lullaby, a song written to lull babies to sleep, but in this case written for the sleepy dormouse in *Alice in Wonderland*. Influenced by Clare and Helen's reading and their knowledge of the form, this poem still contains their voices in its final cautionary advice. Notice also how they have enjoyed presenting their poem.

Dormouse's Lullaby

Rock-a-bye Dormouse,
In the teapot.
Sucking your breack,
And sleeping a lot.
When nightfall comes,
You will climb up the spout.
But do watch out,
'Cause Queenie's about!

by Clare and Helen

Figure 4.4

Further reading

Rosen, M. (1989) *Did I Hear You Write?* London: Andre Deutsch.
Sedgwick, F. (1997) *Read my Mind: Young Children, Poetry and Learning.* London: Routledge.

NON-NARRATIVE WRITING

> At all key stages more children choose to write narrative rather than non-narrative and generally the standard of writing is higher in narrative.
> (QCA, 1998; p. 14)

This statement shows how important it is to give children a broad experience of writing non-narrative, as well as narrative. For many children narrative may be the easier form to manipulate, but by giving them a range of different experiences and support, non-narrative writing can become more attainable and more purposeful.

As has been said, non-narrative writing in primary schools covers a range of purposes and forms and children need to be given opportunities to write in these, in meaningful contexts, for clearly defined purposes and for specific audiences. In this book there are examples of very young children writing lists, captions and labels. At Key Stages One and Two non-narrative writing occurs across the curriculum as, for example, children label diagrams in science, and write diary accounts in history, captions in geography and instructions in design and technology.

Teaching about genres

Generally, as children move through the key stages, non-narrative features more strongly across the curriculum. To help children learn about different genres of writing it is important for the class teacher to model these for the children. This can be achieved through shared writing, with the whole class or a group, which allows children to investigate the structure, language and purpose of the genre. It is important to have examples of such writing displayed in the classroom for the children to read and explore themselves. Reading and discussing information books will also help children hear and understand the different language patterns and features of texts, as will exposure to information books in group and guided reading sessions. Lewis and Wray (1995) (see opening of this chapter and Chapter 2) argue that the careful support that children need in writing different genres can be provided by 'writing frames' – a series of prompts specific to a genre. In the worked example below, a procedural genre (recipe writing) is being taught. The example demonstrates how a writing frame can be used.

Procedural writing

The procedural genre is one of the easier genres to understand because it records a sequence of events in time (chronologically), and aspects of it can be taught to children of all ages. Procedural writing can cover any set of instructions which uses a series of sequenced steps: instructions for playing a game, using a video recorder or building a model. The *NLS* recommends that in Year 2 children 'write simple instructions, e.g. getting to school, playing a game' and 'use models from reading to organise instructions sequentially . . .'. At Year 5 in the *NLS*, pupils are expected to write '. . . instructions for loading computers, design briefs for technology, rules for games'.

At the beginning of this example a selection of recipes (*NLS*, Year 3.2) is shared with the children and used to explore features of this type of writing. The use of imperative verbs such as 'stir', 'shake,' 'fold' or 'beat', the layout of the text and the use of adverbs in describing how to carry out the actions are all features of this genre which the teacher would focus on. After this initial activity the children, in pairs, could choose their favourite recipe and carry out the following:

- Find the verbs in the recipe. What sort of verbs are used?
- Find the adverbs in the recipe.
- How do you know what quantities to use?
- Which words are used that link with time e.g. 'next', 'then'?

From investigating published recipes children can then move on to being supported in writing their own recipes, initially as a shared writing exercise. At this point an enlarged writing frame is used as a model. A writing frame is a series of prompts specific to the genre so one for a recipe might look like this:

- How to make. . . .
- Ingredients. . . .
- Equipment. . . .
- Method. . . .
  - First
  - Next
  - Next
  - Finally

Now the children go on to individual work with frames. For a child who needs more support additional information can be inserted (e.g. some of the ingredients with quantities); for the more experienced child you could delete prompts under 'Method' shown here. (Full examples of a variety of frames are outlined more fully in the books by Lewis and Wray.)

When the child is using the frame with confidence, recipes can be written independently. Such scaffolded teaching is powered by and is a clear demonstration of Vygotsky's (1978) theory of the zone of proximal development (see Chapter 1).

Many teachers in Key Stage One also teach the procedural genre through the use of recipes, especially after children have been cooking. At this age the work might focus on broader aspects of layout, particularly how the ingredients appear as a list (*National Curriculum*, p. 9). Preliminary activities to 'warm' the genre could include reading and sharing recipes, and sequencing cut-up recipes. With an enlarged version of a favourite recipe a shared text session could be used to ask the children about the different 'sections' in the recipe which are labelled with them. After shared work on an enlarged frame the children could proceed to individual work, this time with a modified version of the one above. For instance, the stages in the method could be numbered.

In summary we have seen children in the examples above:

- clarifying the audience and purpose;
- exploring and discussing different texts, in an interesting and structured way;
- writing the genre alongside the teacher;
- using a frame to support their own writing, either alone or with a partner;
- writing the genre independently.

In the next example a group of Year 5 children use the procedural genre to write an instruction book for a school camera. The handbook had been lost and the class was asked to write new handbooks for different people in the school. This gave the children real audiences and a purpose for doing the writing. One group wrote a handbook for the nursery children and staff, another group for children of their own age, and another wrote (Figure 4.5) for the staff of the school. The teachers had instructed them to make the text simple, straightforward and understandable! As it was Christmas, the children included 'Snappy the Reindeer' to act as guide for the book – an ingenious play on words. The manual was word-processed.

The text makes some use of imperatives, such as 'pull', 'slot' and 'push'. Although laid out in one block, it takes the reader clearly through the sequence of steps required to take a photograph. It might have been more appropriate for the instructions to be laid out in numbered or lettered bullet points which would help the reader follow the instructions. Such support could have been introduced through the use of a writing frame.

In teaching non-narrative writing it is argued that all six genres can be taught using frames and following the same stages outlined above. The last worked example we give is of the report genre which, unlike recount and procedural, is not chronologically organised, and is therefore more demanding.

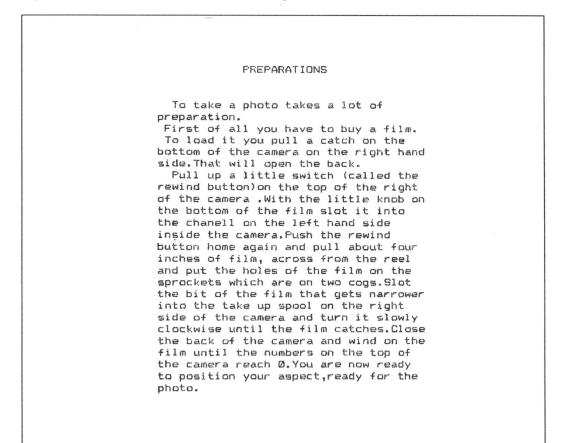

PREPARATIONS

To take a photo takes a lot of preparation.
First of all you have to buy a film.
To load it you pull a catch on the bottom of the camera on the right hand side.That will open the back.
Pull up a little switch (called the rewind button)on the top of the right of the camera .With the little knob on the bottom of the film slot it into the chanell on the left hand side inside the camera.Push the rewind button home again and pull about four inches of film, across from the reel and put the holes of the film on the sprockets which are on two cogs.Slot the bit of the film that gets narrower into the take up spool on the right side of the camera and turn it slowly clockwise until the film catches.Close the back of the camera and wind on the film until the numbers on the top of the camera reach 0.You are now ready to position your aspect,ready for the photo.

Figure 4.5

Report writing

A report usually starts with an overall statement concerning the content of the piece, followed by a description of the specifics including specialist vocabulary or terminology. A report is characterised by generalisations and is usually written in the present tense. In the primary classroom report writing is often asked for in geography or science lessons. Here is an example of a Year 5 child's writing in science:

> Igneous Rocks
> Rocks are sometimes formed from a red-hot liquid that has cooled down and slowly hardened. This type of rock is called igneous. Here are some examples of igneous rock: granite, basalt, diorite, obsian and andesite. Another example of igneous is pumice. It is cooled lava that comes to the surface of the ground. People sometimes use it to clean dry skin off their feet. Granite is a quite a common rock. It is hard, tough cooled molten lava. The speckles are really compact crystals mixed into the lava, which can't be seen to the naked eye. It can be pink, white or grey and sparkly. The whole of Dartmoor is really one big block of granite. But one thing the stones look completely different and I think I know why. It is because the pumice is made on the surface and so it gets more air and that's why it looks bubbly and smooth but granite on the other hand is made under the surface and does not get so much air and that's why it is so solid.

This is a competent piece of writing which demonstrates the way in which a report is structured. It includes an opening general statement, use of technical vocabulary, generalisations and the use throughout of the present tense. You could use such a well structured piece to show the class, perhaps on an OHP in shared text work in the Literacy Hour, how to organise this genre. (As a teacher you would note that the personal tone of the hypothesis at the end is not strictly a feature of reports, but you would nevertheless be pleased to see how writing, thinking and learning unite at this point.)

Taking notes

In the example above the child had to find out about rocks before he composed his report. Such pre-writing activity and research may involve reading information books, searching CD Roms, or exploring the Internet. In such research children need to make notes and this is something they need support with, particularly in overcoming the problem of verbatim copying of facts. The *NLS* states that children need to know the purpose and use of the note taking (Year 5.1). Wray and Lewis (1997, p. 37) remind us that 'to neglect the link between purpose and recording is to risk leaving children feeling that they have to note down all the information they read, even if it is only slightly relevant'.

As with other forms of writing the teacher can model note taking in shared writing with the class. Such modelling could be from a CD Rom or television screen as well as written text and could be reinforced in guided reading and writing sessions. Another way of helping children is through the use of a frame or grid which will help them consider what they already know and what they want to find out. Here is one example of a 'Know, Want, Learn' (KWL) grid with the third column allowing for note taking:

What do I know?	What do I want to find out?	What did I learn?

(Ogle, 1989, in Wray and Lewis, 1997; p. 47)

When reading information texts, children can be shown how to identify words and phrases that are significant. Teacher modelling can illustrate how this can be achieved, using an OHP. After this children can work on their own photocopy, highlighting key words and writing notes in the margin. A further suggestion might be for children to read a piece of information writing and then retell it to a partner in their own words. The important thing in all of this is to keep the link between purpose and recording very clear for the children.

Layout

Children know quite a lot about how texts are laid out from their experiences of writing outside school. Rules for playing games, instructions for assembling Lego models, catalogue pages and video packaging are all very much part of their reading lives. We can build on this implicit knowledge to help children explicitly reflect on the role of organisation and layout in non-fiction writing.

Different types of writing require different layouts and, even though writers may not attend to this aspect in the early stages, knowing about layouts and ultimately using them can aid the organisation of the composition. In your discussions and modelling of layout with children you will of course look at the layout of some narrative texts such as play scripts and poetry where layout plays such an important part; there are also some layouts such as those used for letters which relate to both narrative and non-narrative texts. Some are specific to non-narrative: lists, rules, instructions and so on. Some layouts are very familiar in our society and children will use them with ease; others are not so visible and children will need more inducting into their conventions.

As we saw in the recipe example, layout is an important aspect of some genres, governing, as it does, the reader's expectations. For instance, look back at Figure 4.5 ('Preparations') and consider how much the use of headings and sub-headings and the use of bullet points would have helped the reader. Writing on screen enables layout aspects to be worked on easily.

Cross-curricular links

Most of the examples of writing discussed in this section come from different curriculum areas. Within many of the foundation and core subjects writing is used to help children think and learn, to remember what they have learnt and to give the teacher some evidence to assess their learning. One example of this is seen in Figure 4.6, an explanation of a vehicle designed and made in a Design and Technology lesson.

The diagram gives the reader a clear idea of what the vehicle looks like. It is labelled, with arrows to show the different parts of the vehicle. The text does not have an opening paragraph as most explanations do, but the diagram may act as such.

A subject such as history gives children opportunities to write in a range of genres for different audiences and in different contexts. A topic such as the Victorians will allow older children to write explanations of the growth of the Empire, newspaper reports that argue for the abolition of child labour or discussion papers on whether to have the Great Exhibition or not. The *NLS* states that 'Teachers will need to provide opportunities for practising and applying new skills in independent work at other times. Most of this practice should be productively linked to other curriculum areas' (p. 14).

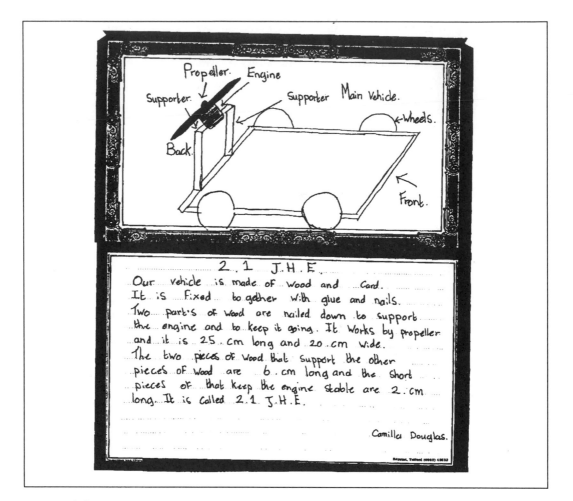

Figure 4.6

Writing in role

One further area to explore is writing in role which allows children to explore imaginary situations and can encourage them to write in new genres. Writing in role allows young writers to feel a real need and purpose for writing; it gives them a strong context for writing and empowers them to write for a real (albeit imaginary) audience. Taking on writing in another role is a possible follow-up from reading or from drama.

Writing after reading

One of the most productive contexts for working on non-narrative is, paradoxically, the context of a story. A text such as *Mrs Plug the Plumber* (Allan Ahlberg and Joe Wright) could stimulate writing activities such as:

- a catalogue of a plumber's equipment, labelled and in alphabetical order;
- safety notices for certain pieces of equipment e.g. the blowlamp;
- a leaflet to advertise Mrs Plug's services;

- tickets for the world cruise and luggage labels;
- a note to cancel the milk;
- a postcard home from the Plugs.

Figure 4.7 is an example of the postcard which Elloa has written using the information that she gained from the story. (The address was clearly scribed on the reverse of the card.) She is writing in role as Mrs Plug although she does not completely sustain it as we see when she switches into her own name as she signs off.

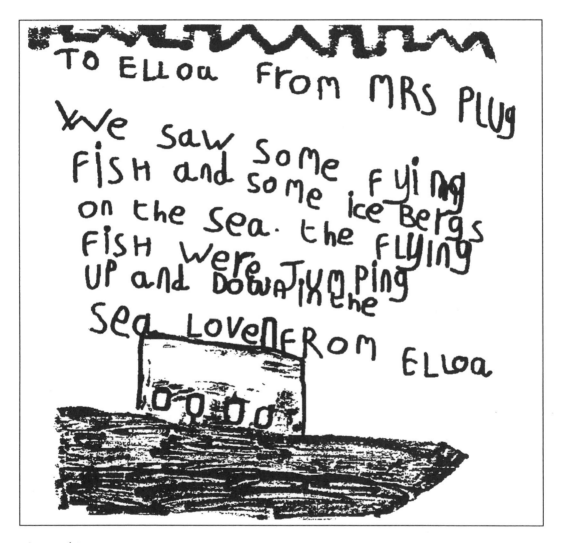

Figure 4.7

The story has enabled Elloa to write in a generic form, in this case a 'recount' which is quite a comfortable genre for children as it is often personal and about people and events familiar to them (see Chapter 2). She uses 'I' and 'we' and the past tense, all generic features of recount, and not difficult to manage because of the clear links with writing in the first person narrative.

All stories can give opportunities for genuinely contextualised writing in non-narrative genres. At Key Stage Two, a novel such as *The Runaways* (Ruth Thomas) could give rise to writing a missing persons' poster, a newspaper article about the missing children and a police report on progress in the investigation so far. From *The Wreck of the Zanzibar* (Michael Morpurgo) there are opportunities for persuasive writing, promoting the grandmother's and Laura's view that the turtle should not be eaten, and procedural writing in the form of instructions on how to reach the Scilly Isles.

Writing after drama

> Under some circumstances children do seem able to write in the kinds of genres that genre theorists regard as socially important. It is observable, for instance, that children writing in role, either as part of a drama or in what might be termed 'drama on paper' can take on voices that they never usually use, and write as politicians, scientists or news reporters.
> Myra Barrs (1994, pp. 255–6)

The Volcano, Learning through Drama (ILEA, 1985) is a drama resource pack that places children on an island with an active volcano. Each child takes on a character who lives on the island which they develop. A crisis occurs as the volcano starts to erupt; the islanders all decide to leave except for one who stays to look after the animals. After carrying out the initial drama, a class of Year 5 children, with total involvement and commitment to the drama, wrote in a variety of styles and forms. The first example (Figure 4.8), a flier from the tourist office, is a piece of writing that had been written before the eruption, intended to encourage eco-tourists to visit the island.

This is another example of the persuasion genre, here organised in the form of an advertisement. The piece is written for tourists who want a quiet environmentally friendly place to visit and the flier suggests the island has 'no pollution' and 'a wide range of wild life'. Such a piece could have been developed further by reading travel brochures to understand the language and structure that are often used to encourage tourists.

The next example is a word-processed newspaper report from *The Daily Scoop*.

> The islanders of Passamquddy fled in terror from the volcano, Mississippi. The Mississippi last erupted in 1928, over 60 years ago. The Mayor held a meeting on the subject last Monday. It was decided that the island should be evacuated but a 16 year old girl named Geraldine Harris said she would not be forced to leave Passamquddy. Geraldine is now living on Passamquddy alone. On leaving Passamquddy a boat went down off the coast of South America. Geraldine is quite sure that Mississippi will not erupt so she will be quite safe.

Finally a child in role as Bert Robinson, the butcher, wrote to the only islander who remained on the island. His letter, Figure 4.9, is a mixture of persuasion and recount genres.

There were many more examples written after just one morning's drama. The children were stimulated and eager to write as the project allowed them to explore writing within an imaginative framework which gave them a real purpose and audience. Although such lengthy drama work cannot be attempted within the structure of the Literacy Hour, the follow-up writing can be.

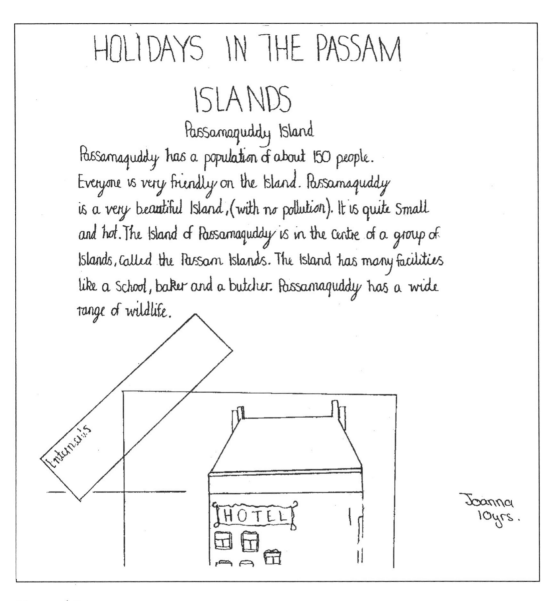

Figure 4.8

It is important that young writers of non-fiction understand the links between reading and writing, and from this they will begin to understand the structure and form of different types of writing. With appropriate support, children will move on to writing the genres independently for themselves. When children come to understand the purpose of the task, they will appreciate and enjoy the craft of non-narrative writing.

Many of the ideas in this chapter intended to aid children's composition in narrative, poetry and non-narrative writing are explored because young writers need encouragement to produce and shape writing, especially in new forms and especially when the transcription elements in the writing process have not yet become automatic. The role of the teacher is clear: she keeps the composition process going from 'warm-ups', through discussion, sharing of information and key words; she helps with

24 Mathale
Flamingo
Brazil
28 March 1900

Dear Geraldine
                    You can't imagine
how concerned I feel about
you. Are you sure you won't
change your mind and leave
because we could still send
out a boat?
I am now living in Brazil
with Judy and little baby Tom.
The other people that were
on the Island have gone
to England and Canada.
I do hope that the volcano
won't explode and we hope
to se you soon.
                    love from
                    Mr Bert Robinsoon
                    the butcher

Figure 4.9

clarifying form, purpose and audience; she provides prompts and interest during the
writing; she helps with revision; she shows respect and pleasure when the work is

finished. Composition is at the heart of writing and the creative process is at the root of many of the most important activities that humans engage in. We need to nurture these impulses and ensure our writers leave the primary school as eager to compose in writing in every sphere as they normally are in their speaking.

Further reading

Graves, D. (1989) *Investigate Non-Fiction*. Portsmouth: Heinemann.
Wray, D. and Lewis, M. (1997) *Extending Literacy: Children's Reading and Writing Non-Fiction*. London: Routledge.

CHAPTER 5

Transcription: Spelling, Punctuation and Handwriting

Alison Kelly

> My earliest memories of writing, and the only thoughts that still remain from my primary
> school days, are of continually repeating letters and words in set spaces, making sure that all
> the letters were the same size. . . .
> (Year 1 undergraduate on BA[QTS] course)

This is the experience of many children – that writing is just about the physical aspects
of spelling, handwriting and punctuation. You will remember that Chapter 2 introduced
the distinction between 'composition' and 'transcription' and that in Chapter 4 we took
a careful look at supporting composition. These earlier chapters discussed the
importance of ensuring that children have a balanced view of the writing process and
are aware of the importance of the content of their writing as well as its 'presentation'
as the *National Curriculum* describes it. But now we do turn to the secretarial aspects
of writing: spelling, handwriting and punctuation, which are, of course, very important.

SPELLING

> The aim should be that by the end of compulsory schooling pupils should be able to spell
> confidently most of the words that they are likely to need to use frequently in their writing; to
> recognise those aspects of English spelling that are systematic; to make a sensible attempt to
> spell words that they have not seen before; to check their work for misspellings and to use a
> dictionary appropriately. The aim cannot be the correct unaided spelling of any English word
> – there are too many words in English that can catch out even the best speller.
> (Cox, 1991; p. 148)

This quote is taken from the discussion paper which formed the basis of the English
National Curriculum. It is a useful and realistic reminder of what we want to achieve
with the children we teach. As it suggests, this is a challenging area, not least because
of the complexity of our spelling system. There are 26 letters in the alphabet but at least
44 single sounds (phonemes) that those letters have to represent and, as this famous
(or infamous) little snatch of poetry shows, some of them have to work overtime!

> I take it you already know
> Of tough and bough and cough and dough?
> Others may stumble but not you,
> On hiccough, thorough, laugh and through.
> (in Rosen, 1995; p. 36)

One difficulty lies with the alphabet used for English, which is not one that was
intended to fit English sounds. Its history can be traced back over thousands of years
and thousands of miles to 1700 BC in the Middle East, where a North Semitic language,
like Hebrew, was spoken. This alphabet was passed from the Phoenicians to the

Greeks, whose model influenced the Etruscans, who, in turn, influenced the Romans. Christian missionaries arrived in this country in the sixth century and brought the Roman alphabet with them (Crystal, 1995). As you will see in the section below on Etymology, our language has also been profoundly influenced by the different groups of people who have settled here over the centuries all bringing with them their own languages. All of this makes for a rich but sometimes bewildering linguistic potpourri and one where fewer than half of common English words have regular sound–symbol correspondence.

This chapter looks at ways of teaching spelling that encourage children to inspect words with care and interest and that help them see where there are regularities. But before that we look at recent concerns that have been raised about the teaching of spelling. Then we look at what we know of how children learn to spell and what teachers need to know about spelling at their own level in order to support children in the best possible ways.

Concerns about the teaching of Spelling

As the Introduction and Chapter 1 in this book show, early approaches to writing focussed exclusively on transcriptional aspects at the expense of composition. Rote learning and copying were the order of the day. By the 1960s, the pendulum had swung back with the 'creative writing' movement, where all the focus seemed to be on the production of imaginative writing. A teacher then was quoted as saying that 'spelling is learned naturally by the children and, from the reading, punctuation becomes increasingly familiar' (quoted in Clegg, 1964; p. 40). This idea that, for some children, spelling can be learned 'naturally' is one that recurs from time to time and Margaret Peters' research into spelling (first published in 1967, revised edition 1985) gave us a neat soundbite for this with the title of her book *Spelling: Caught or Taught?* Peters cites evidence of challenges (and counter-challenges) to the systematic teaching of spelling from the very beginnings of this century, and the more recent writing 'process' movement and 'developmental' or 'emergent' approaches to writing have been criticised for marginalising the teaching of the presentational skills of writing.

Writing process approaches

Let us start with the writing process movement (see Chapter 2) which drew teachers' attention to the composition/transcription distinction and suggested that it was necessary for children to be clear about that separation too. A teacher's prompting that children should, in the first instance, concentrate on getting the ideas down without worrying about the spellings is indeed a worrying one if that was all that was going on. But for many, such advice was seen only as the first step in the process of writing and the children would go on to 'edit' their work paying proper attention to the spelling and other surface skills of writing. It could be that the separation of composition and transcription, with the apparent relegation of transcription to second place, led to some misunderstandings about the importance teachers were placing upon it. This may have been the case for some teachers, but many carefully attended to the teaching of spelling and handwriting.

'Developmental/emergent' approaches

The tension between composition and transcription is possibly most visible for a very young writer when the strain of forming letters and spelling words can seriously inhibit the fluency of writing. This is why routines such as dictated writing (see Chapter 3), which allow a focus on composition, are so important in the early years.

As we showed in Chapter 2, research into children's early moves into literacy revealed how they can make active and creative hypotheses about ways in which all of the writing system works. Remind yourself by looking at Figure 5.1, Madeleine's representation of her first day at play group.

Figure 5.1

As well as drawing the teacher and children, she has 'written' their names underneath. She knows that drawing and writing are different; that they look different and that they have different functions. Arriving alongside insights about composition and transcription, such findings had exciting potential for work in the early years. It became clear that encouraging children to make unaided spelling guesses not only showed teachers what the children knew and understood about writing but it also freed children from the transcriptional strain of 'getting it right' at the first attempt. They were enabled to focus on what it was they wanted to say. So the suggestion that children should 'have-a-go' at their spellings stems from a concern to 'free up' composition.

At about the same time, interesting research was being published about the nature of the children's invented spellings. For instance, the work of Ferreiro and Teberosky

(1979), two researchers who were influenced by Piaget's work, suggested that children go through stages in their writing and that it is possible to describe a developmental progression. *The Beginnings of Writing* (Temple *et al.*, 1982) was read by many teachers and reinforced the idea of spelling stages. We will return to the idea of spelling stages below but the important point is that the idea of stages can be interpreted as suggesting that there is a natural progression and this can marginalise the teacher's role. The danger then with labels like 'developmental' or 'emergent' is that they might suggest that the teacher can simply let it all happen and does not need to do any specific teaching. The notion of stages also suggests a rigidity and uniformity in children's learning and that all children will pass through the same stages in the same way. Teachers know that this is not the case!

How do children learn to spell?

Some children appear to learn to spell quite easily without any apparent spelling lessons and one source of anxiety for teachers about their role could rest with an implicit view that somehow we are born as 'good' or 'bad' spellers. Such a view can leave the teacher feeling uneasy about the effectiveness of her teaching so it is helpful to know what does contribute to the success of some children. This is what Margaret Peters (1985) looked at in her study of children who appeared to have 'caught' spelling. She found that verbal ability and interest in words, good visual perception and what she terms 'carefulness' in handwriting were important factors in the children's success (p. 21). Such research provides helpful classroom pointers and we shall look at practical activities which support the development of these factors in the sections below on teaching spelling and handwriting.

Spelling development

Another area we know much more about now concerns spelling development. New knowledge about spelling development has enabled teachers to identify what counts as spelling progress. Research into early literacy (e.g. Clay, 1975; Bissex, 1980; Goodman, 1984) has yielded fascinating insights into the very beginnings of spelling development, and knowing about these early stages can inform our teaching considerably. One commonly used model of spelling development comes from Richard Gentry (1982), who identifies five possible stages. His work is based on the case study of a single child (Bissex, 1980), which means that we do need to approach it with some caution! The labels he uses for the different stages describe what the child is doing, not the teacher. As we said above, the notion of stages can be a very beguiling one and it is most important that we use this understanding flexibly and do not treat them as neat staging posts through which every child will pass in just the same way. Here is a brief summary of some of the features of Gentry's stages:

1. *Pre-communicative*
- knows that symbols can be used to say something;
- uses a range of symbols (invented, numbers, letters – upper and lower case);
- does not make sound–symbol connections.

2. *Semi-phonetic*
- is beginning to make sound–symbol connections;
- knows about word boundaries, how writing is arranged on a page;
- may shorten some words.

3. *Phonetic*
- uses sound–symbol connections consistently;
- uses known words (sight vocabulary).

4. *Transitional*
- uses visual strategies;
- uses most conventions of spelling system.

5. *Correct*
- has basic knowledge of spelling system and rules;
- knows about word structure (morphology);
- has a large sight vocabulary.

If we look at the progress of one child across her first year in school we can see what aspects of these stages actually look like. First, a word about the context of these pieces. They were written by Kelly when she was five years old and attending a primary school in South-East London. She was a confident and outgoing child, neither an over- nor an under-achiever. It was part of the school's assessment policy that samples of children's writing would be kept regularly and be passed from teacher to teacher in a portfolio (see Chapter 6). The samples were to be 'unaided' (i.e. containing the children's own spelling attempts) so that both composition and presentation could be monitored. Such unaided writing was only a part of the writing curriculum in this reception class. Shared writing, copying, dictated writing, spelling and handwriting were all regular classroom routines and it is important to remember this when looking at the examples below as such development came about as part of well structured and carefully focussed teaching. There is much to be said about the composition of Kelly's pieces but the focus of this chapter is spelling. The reminder about content is important though and in this classroom the teacher was most rigorous in responding to the content of the pieces as well as to the presentational aspects. Finally, the intention of presenting these pieces here is to illustrate spelling development; I will look at practical issues concerning the nature of our responses to such early attempts in a later section.

In her first week at school Kelly (age 5.3) wrote the story in Figure 5.2:

> The fox in the wood. What can he see? Some ducks playing in the pond. A little boy called
> Sean came along. The little boy said 'Get away you nasty fox.' The fox ran away and the boy
> said to the ducks 'Don't be afraid, I am only a little boy.'
> (as dictated to her teacher).

This is an example of Gentry's 'pre-communicative writing' in that there is no apparent evidence of sound–symbol correlation. The label 'pre-communicative' is slightly misleading as she clearly is communicating meaning but remember that 'pre-communicative' is a label for the spelling. (You might find 'pre-phonemic', as used by Temple *et al.*, 1982, a more useful label.) However, she already knows quite a lot about the presentational aspects of spelling: she knows writing runs from left to right and is arranged on the page in lines; she knows that writing consists of strings of letters (but not that these are divided up into units – words – yet) and that the same letters can be

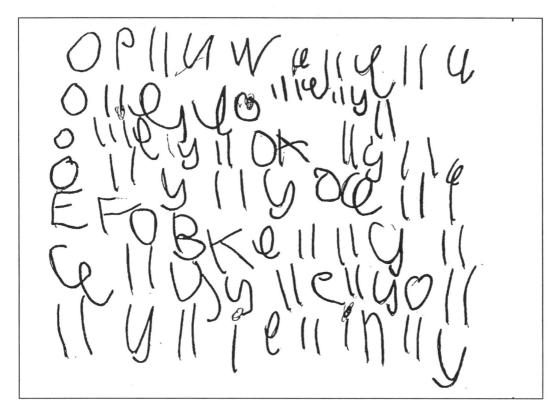

Figure 5.2

used in different combinations. In common with many young writers she draws heavily on the most familiar of all strings of letters at this point – her name.

As an important aside, compare Kelly's work with that of a bilingual child, Shirin, in the same class, as seen in Figure 5.3.

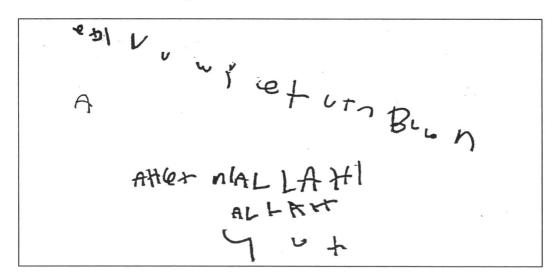

Figure 5.3

This was Shirin's response to her teacher's request to write something about her holiday. A fluent Urdu speaker, the writing shows what a remarkable amount Shirin has already grasped about two quite separate writing systems. She started with the top line which ran from right to left and includes distinctive characters influenced by the Urdu alphabet. When she went on to write 'Allah' on the next line she uses the characters of the English alphabet written from left to right. Such early attempts need to be recognised, applauded and built upon. In this case, the teacher went on to make a book with Shirin who dictated what she wanted it to say to the teacher and then her father was enlisted to translate it into Urdu. These two versions allowed the teacher to build on the child's mother tongue while supporting her development in reading and writing English.

Back to Kelly who, a month later, wrote the caption in Figure 5.4 for a picture:

I am in the garden and my friend is in the garden and we found a frog. The frog hopped away.

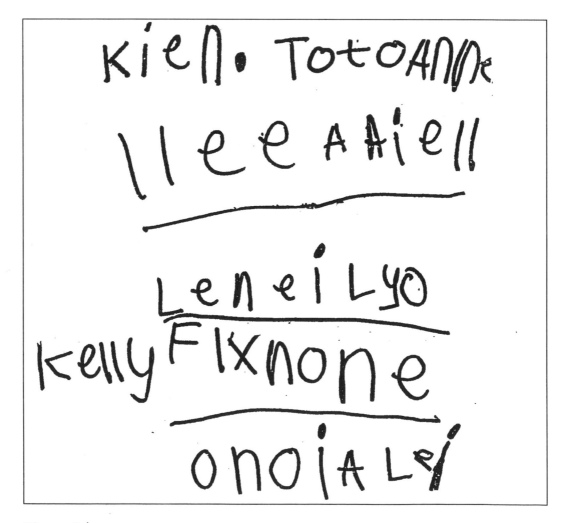

Figure 5.4

Although this is still 'pre-communicative', you will see that Kelly has made considerable progress in her understanding. Most importantly she seems to be moving towards the concept of words, as the underlining and the relished full stop after 'kien' suggest. There are words she can spell, 'To', 'to' and 'Anne' (her friend's name), and she is using a greater range of letters.

In December she makes a most significant leap with the reply in Figure 5.5 to her teacher's 'post-it' on a message board enquiring about Kelly's weekend plans. She replies:

My friend's coming tomorrow and we are going to play with each other.

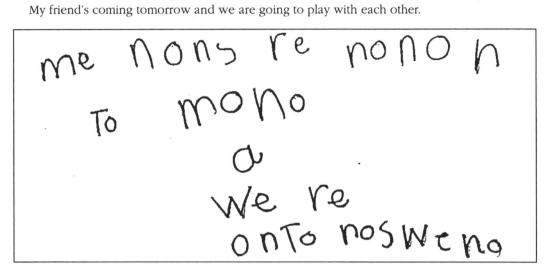

Figure 5.5

We see here the beginnings of sound-symbol correspondence. This is what Gentry terms 'semi-phonetic' writing. Look, for instance, at her attempt of 'tomorrow' – 'to mono'. There are sight words in use too: 'to' and 'we'. The use of 're' for 'are' is characteristic of this stage where the child draws on the name of the letter – 'R' – (for that is what she hears). Importantly though, the 'e' at the end 're' shows that she is not only making use of sound strategies but also using the look of the word; we cannot hear the 'e' on the end of 'are', we see it on the page. There is an important point to be made here about links between reading and writing. It seems that children begin to represent individual sounds or phonemes in their writing with such intent concentration that there is a knock-on effect for their reading. Recent research (Goswami, 1995) shows how children's attempts at writing words help crystallise the concept of the phoneme, thus enhancing phonemic awareness, an important underpinning for effective use of phonic strategies in reading.

The next piece (Figure 5.6), written in February, is a caption for a drawing:

I like this flower because it smells nice and it is lovely.

There is a real attempt here to spell each word relying mostly on the sounds, especially initial ones. She is no longer using letter names. Apart from the omission of 'is' in the last line, there is one-to-one correspondence (i.e. matching of spoken and written

I ILK THIS
FnonBue chP
It ShEl nonoy
AnD It noeLLo

Figure 5.6

units), there is more evidence of sight words and, in the brave attempt at 'because', evidence of sight strategies – she knows there is a 'u' in there somewhere! She is on the way to the 'phonetic' stage where there is an attempt to represent each sound.

The final sample from this year is the first page of a story (Figure 5.7) written in June, which shows Kelly continuing to progress:

> One day there was a little boy who wanted a little bear but his mummy wouldn't let him have one. 'Then I'll be upset,' said the little boy.

She continues to use phonic strategies ('likl booe'), sight strategies ('sid' for 'said') and known words. The fact that she resorts to the earlier strategy of using her name when really stuck – see her last attempt at 'boy' ('belly') – is a useful reminder of the fluidity of these early writing stages and the fact that children do move backwards as well as forward! The important thing is to be able to recognise the strategies being used so that you can respond appropriately.

One dey ThcR Yes a
liki Booe wcDo WELa
iiKi BELR BeT HeS
MyMMy WELoT LOVT
HeM Hellone Then
Sid The liKi Bel i
WELL BeH 4P SLok
① Sdd The liKi BElly

Figure 5.7

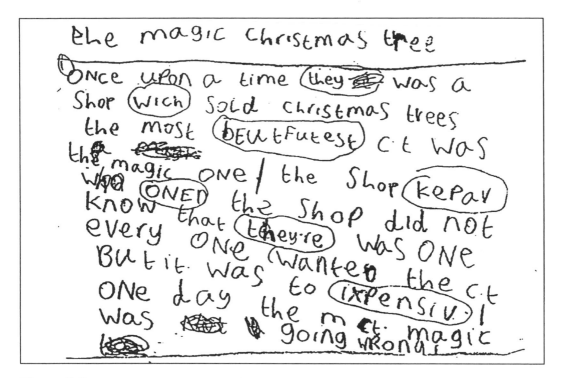

Figure 5.8

Gentry's final stages are 'transitional' and 'correct'. A transitional speller will be using vowels in each syllable and beginning to develop visual strategies. We have evidence of Kelly doing the latter but not the former. In Figure 5.8 a Year 2 child is showing a confident grasp of aspects of the transitional stage.

Note the spellings of polysyllabic words such as 'beautifulest', 'keeper' and 'expensive'. (Two other points of interest are the circled words being the ones that she has identified as needing help with and the use of the initials 'ct' for 'Christmas tree' which stems from class discussion about drafting techniques.)

Learning styles

It is clear from looking at the transcripts and tone of Kelly's work that she is a confident young writer; this is not the case for all children and we do need to take account of what we know about children's different learning styles when we plan our teaching. A longitudinal study by Bussis *et al.* (in Barrs and Thomas, 1991) has illuminated our understanding about this. Focussing mainly on reading, it revealed children whose overall learning style was one that favoured 'big shapes' (the pattern and language of the texts) while others went for 'smaller units' (words and sounds). The former group tended to be risk takers as they went for the overall meaning and fluency of a text, sometimes at the expense of word for word accuracy. Those who went for the smaller units were not such confident risk takers preferring a step by step approach as they tackled individual words and letters. Bussis' findings suggested that such learning styles were not restricted to reading and extended to other curriculum areas and it seems highly likely that the same findings will apply to the confidence with which children approach spelling tasks. In the section on spelling strategies we look at ways of developing children's confidence. More recent research (Dombey and Moustafa, 1998) suggests that difference in learning styles also extends to whether the children initially draw from visual or aural data. The important issue here is to take on board these different learning styles and to be mindful of Bussis' finding that, provided the teacher was offering a balanced teaching 'mix' which addressed all aspects of reading, then the children were not disadvantaged by their learning style. So when we come to think about planning, it is most important that we structure it to include a balance of strategies.

What do teachers need to know about spelling?

From discussion so far, we know that while some children appear to take to spelling with ease this is not the case for most of them. As the Cox quote at the beginning of the chapter reminds us, there are spellings to daunt even the most confident of spellers, and spelling, taught well, should be an intriguing area for everyone. So we need to give explicit spelling lessons to all. We know that children learn in different ways and that our teaching needs to take account of this, particularly with regard to encouraging children to take risks and in providing a broad range of strategies. We know that learning to spell is a developmental process and that there are some broad indicative stages through which young writers seem to pass (but not necessarily in a smooth or sequential way). In this section we look at some of the spelling lessons we have to give ourselves in order to teach children effectively.

Spelling rules

The whole business of spelling rules is fraught with difficulty partly because of the inconsistencies in our language and partly because they are sometimes just very hard to understand. This one seems simple enough: 'there will be a double "l", "f" or "s" after a single vowel at the end of a short word (e.g. fuss, tell, sniff)', but then there are the exceptions 'us', 'bus', 'gas', 'if', 'of', 'this', 'yes': to name a few. Others are more extended and, therefore, harder for young children to get their heads round: 'Words ending in both a single vowel and a single consonant always double the last consonant before adding an ending beginning with a vowel (e.g. stop, stopped, stopping)' (rules taken from Bannatyne and Cotterell, 1966).

Rules are only useful when they apply to a large number of words, when there are few exceptions and when they are easily understood. Mike Torbe (1995) suggests that the following might be helpful; he calls them 'descriptions' rather than rules.

1. 'q' is always followed by 'u' and another vowel always follows the 'u';
2. 'i' (pronounced 'eye') at the end of words is spelled 'y' or (less often) 'igh';
3. words that sound as if they have an 'o' in them generally spell it with 'oa' in the middle of the word and 'ow' at the end;
4. words that sound as if they have an 'a' in them generally spell it 'ai' in the middle and 'ay' at the end;
5. English words do not end with 'i', 'o', 'u', 'j' or 'v'. Instead they follow these patterns: i = ie or y, o = ow, u = ue, j = ge or dge, v = ve;

6. the 'er' sound at the end of words is generally spelled 'er';
7. when you add 'full' to the end of a word, it drops one 'l' and becomes 'ful'.
(Torbe, 1995; pp. 77–8)

What is maybe more helpful is a general rule about English spelling which concerns the fixed units that contribute to words and stay constant. We can understand this better if we know about morphology (the structure of words) and etymology (the history of words). Both these areas reveal consistencies that will help you to teach clearly, to respond in a focussed and useful way to children's spelling mistakes and to make informed plans for teaching spelling. The section on 'Spelling Conventions and Rules' for Key Stage 2 in the *NLS* framework draws heavily from these areas of understanding. The section below on Teaching Spelling includes teaching suggestions for addressing the issues raised in this section. There is a glossary at the end of this chapter to remind you of some of the terminology you need to know.

Morphology

Morphology is the study of the structure of words. It is an area that we need to know about explicitly because it enables us to help children see unchanging patterns in spelling. Let us take the word 'teach' which is the root of 'teacher', 'teaching' and 'unteachable'. The bits that come before and after words are called affixes. There are two sorts of affix: prefixes which come before the root and suffixes which come after the root. So in the word 'unteachable', 'un-' is a prefix and '-able' is a suffix. (It helps to know that 'pre' comes from Latin and means 'before' and the 'su' in suffix comes from the Latin 'sub' meaning 'under'.)

Affixes work in two ways: inflectionally and derivationally. Inflectional suffixes (and they are always suffixes) show changes in meaning and mark grammatical contrasts. The main inflectional endings in English are as follows:

- plural   e.g. dog*s*
- to mark possession   e.g. the dog'*s* collar, the dogs*'* collars
- regular verbs
  the past tense   e.g. I walk*ed*
  past participle   e.g. I have walk*ed*
  present tense, 3rd person singular   e.g. she walk*s*
  present participle   e.g. walk*ing*
- comparatives and superlatives   e.g. bright, bright*er*, bright*est*.

There are exceptions to all of these and you will find that children's errors frequently demonstrate their over-generalisation of such endings; for instance, in writing 'mouses' instead of the irregular plural 'mice'. Another difficulty that children may encounter with inflectional endings is the fact that they sound different; try saying 'ripped', 'pinned' and 'plodded' and you will hear the same -ed ending sounding as '-t', '-d' and '-id' respectively. Plurals can be heard differently too as you can see in a child's spelling of 'dogz'. There is more consistency between the look of words than there is between their sounds. The '-ed' remains constant in writing despite changes in pronunciation. The important thing for children to know is that it is the meaning that is privileged over and above the sound of the word.

'Derivational affixes' are used to create new words; they both add and change meaning. Adding the prefix 'un-' and the suffix '-able' to 'teach' makes for a total change of meaning! It is interesting for you (and older children) to note that a derivational suffix changes the word class of the root it is added to, but a derivational prefix does not. So the addition of the suffix '-er' to 'teach' changes the verb 'teach' into the noun 'teacher'. On the other hand, while the prefix 'un-' changes the meaning of 'happy' it has not changed the word class: 'happy' and 'unhappy' are both adjectives.

One of the challenges of linguistic study is that no sooner do you get affixes and roots sorted out than you learn that they are also termed morphemes! These are the smallest parts of words, 'the elements out of which words can be constructed' (Crystal, 1995; p. 198). Maybe they are best understood as little chunks that make meaning and that cannot be broken down further. There are two sorts: 'free morphemes', which are just that, free to stand on their own ('teach', 'dog', 'talk'), and 'bound morphemes', which have to be bound or tied to another morpheme to make sense. Inflectional suffixes such as the 's' in 'dogs' and the 'ed' in 'talked' are bound morphemes as are the prefix and suffix in '*un*teach*able*'.

Etymology

Etymology is about the history of words. It explains the connections between words; for instance 'telephone', 'television', 'telepathy' and 'telegraph' all share the same prefix, 'tele-', which comes from Greek and means 'at a distance'. Etymology is a fascinating and rich area that can really engage children's interest and stimulate their curiosity. It is an area of study that demands that we know a little about the history of the English language itself. This history is about the many different groups of people who arrived and settled here across the centuries. They brought their own languages and we can find traces of these in English today. The chart in Figure 5.9 provides you with an overview of these influences. (The word examples are taken from Mudd, 1997.)

HISTORY OF THE ENGLISH LANGUAGE

DATE	INFLUENCES	WORDS STILL IN USE
500 BC	Celtic tribes speaking different dialects.	crag, whisky
43AD - 410AD	Romans invade and settle. Latin becomes official language of government, Celtic languages persist.	
350 - 600	Angles, Saxons and Jutes invade. Old English (OE) develops from their Germanic dialects.	house, mother, farm, love
600 - 700	Anglo-Saxons converted to Christianity; Latin becomes more influential.	candle, bishop, mass
500 - 800	OE written down using Latin alphabet which did not have symbols for some sounds e.g. 'th'. OE spoken in different dialects, Celtic and Latin also spoken.	
800	Viking invasion (from Scandanavia) and settlements begin, bringing Old Norse with them.	sky, egg, cake, anger
871-899	King Alfred develops use of English to promote national identity; records, literature written in English. Some Latin works translated.	
1066	Norman invasion - French becomes language of court, ruling classes, government; Latin still used in church, OE still spoken.	court, castle, prison, tax
1100 - 1500	'Middle' English develops from French influence	
1362	King's speech at opening of parliament made in English	
1387	Chaucer's *Canterbury Tales* written in English	
1300 - 1600	Standard English begins to develop out of East Midlands dialect (used by universities, court, government). First grammar books written.	
1476	Caxton's printing press contributes to standardisation	'gh' introduced e.g. ghost
Renaissance	Renewed 'importation' of Greek and Latin words with learning revived	'dette' becomes 'debt' (from Latin 'debitum'
1755	Samuel Johnson's dictionary fixes spellings for the first time	
1870	Education Act makes education compulsory for all, with Standard English demanded at school.	

Examples taken from Mudd, N. (1997) The Power of Words Royston :UKRA

Figure 5.9

One of the most exciting aspects of this subject is the way that understanding a little history reveals how dynamic language is; it never sits still, as the addition of 'Teletubbies' to our stock of 'tele-' words demonstrates!

Our language is full of borrowed (loan) words like 'cafe' (French), 'bungalow' (Hindi) and tycoon (Japanese). We add words (neologisms) all the time: 'internet', 'icon'; the Oxford English Dictionary has an 'Addenda' section for these. Then there are acronyms like AIDS (Aquired Immune Deficiency Syndrome), INSET (In-service Training) and SCUBA (Self-Contained Underwater Breathing Apparatus).

Spelling strategies

If we think back to Kelly, we saw a young child drawing from many different sources as she grappled with the complexity of the spelling system. The nature of our language means that spellers need to draw from a wide pool of linguistic knowledge. We do, of course, rely partly on the sounds and on the look of the whole word too (and remember that the extent to which children do this may depend on their learning style).

But what about breaking words down to make spelling easier? Some experts (e.g. Torbe, 1995) suggest splitting words into syllables but others (e.g. Ramsden, 1993) feel this is not always helpful. Rules about syllabification are by no means straightforward and segmenting a word into syllables can lead to sounding out which is not always reliable. However, as the sections on morphology and etymology showed, there are other ways of segmenting words that relate to meaning and may be more helpful.

Recent research has given us another, more child-friendly way of splitting words up: into their 'onsets' and 'rimes'. Many words, such as 'bread' and 'tread', can be broken down into an onset (the opening consonant or consonant cluster e.g. 'br', 'tr') and rime (the vowel sound and any other consonants; the unit which rhymes e.g. 'ead'). Several researchers (Bryant and Bradley, 1985; Goswami and Bryant, 1991; Goswami, 1995) have investigated the importance of children's early phonemic awareness and the impact this has later on their ability to use phonic strategies. These researchers show that early experience of rhyme (through nursery rhymes, rhyming books etc.) lays important foundations for phonemic awareness. These foundations are established as children draw on their experience of rhyme to make rime analogies which draw their attention to phonemes. So a child may be able to link the words 'man', 'van', 'pan' and 'can' because she can hear the shared rime ('-an'). In Figure 5.10 a five year old enjoys the power of onset swapping!

Figure 5.10

Onsets and rimes provide a way of seeing regularities between words that are more reliable than sound strategies. Goswami (1995) tells us that there are 90 words that share the 'ight' rime, while common rimes such as 'en' (in 'ten') and 'an' (in 'fan') have a staggering 904 and 750 respectively!

To conclude then we have to draw from a range of features when we spell. These are listed below with an indication of where they appear in the National Curriculum Programmes of Study for Writing:

- the look of the word (Key Stages One and Two);
- the sounds in the word (Key Stages One and Two);
- common letter strings (Key Stage One) e.g. -ough. . . . ;
- knowing that groups of words are linked by meaning (Key Stage Two) e.g. fact, factual, finite, definite, infinite;
- inflectional endings (Key Stage Two) e.g. flapp*ed,* glid*ed,* soar*ed;*
- rime analogies e.g. m*ight,* f*ight,* l*ight,* c*at,* b*at,* r*at;*
- etymology (Key Stage Two) e.g. tele- (Greek) meaning 'far' e.g. telephone, television, telegram;
- prefixes and suffixes (Key Stages One and Two) e.g. im-, bi, -ed, -ing.

Teaching spelling

When?

You will need to plan opportunities for teaching spelling into your regular routines such as shared reading and writing (see Chapter 3). As well as using these to introduce new work, (for instance looking at inflectional 'ed' endings in a story), these routines provide ideal opportunities for consolidating and reinforcing previous work. Some of your teaching will arise more incidentally from ongoing pieces of writing as the children work on editing, and you may identify a number of common difficulties that you choose to tackle in a specially planned whole-class or group session. Spelling also lends itself well to short sharp bursts of teaching; maybe a quick five minutes focussing on a word many children are finding hard – 'because' is always a good contender! Draw the class together to look closely at the word, identify its particular difficulties, highlight these, maybe make up a class mnemonic ('bears eat cakes and unpack suitcases early'), and draw analogies with another word – 'cause'. Regular slots like these, taken at a good pace, can tackle individual difficulties and generally raise the children's interest in words.

Spelling will be addressed, along with phonics, during Word level work in the Literacy Hour. In Key Stage One this takes the form of fifteen minutes whole-class work. In addition to this, the twenty minute group work slot may include spelling activities, either with the teacher or working independently. The same model applies to Key Stage Two although the whole-class slot is shared between Word and Sentence level work.

How? Four more 'rules'

How to go about teaching spelling? The first rule is – positively! Spelling is an area of enormous anxiety for many children so the quality and tone of our response to their attempts is important. Look back to Figure 5.8 and the child's guesses for 'which'/ 'wich', 'beautifulest'/ 'beutfutest' and 'expensive'/ 'ixpensiv'. In each case she has got more of the word right than wrong; children will be most encouraged when this is pointed out to them. As well as engendering a more positive attitude this also focusses the children's attention on the different parts of the word; having identified what they have got right they are then encouraged to look with care at the part of the word that is wrong.

Closely tied to this comes the second rule: encourage the children's interest and curiosity in words. Enthusiastic teaching can offer the children a model of spelling as a topic that is fascinating, not fearful. Many of the activities below encourage the children to find out about words, their history and their make-up. Activities that focus on the regular features of language such as prefixes and suffixes (see teaching ideas on these below) will be most supportive in enabling children to see regularities and consistencies and increase their curiosity and confidence.

Thirdly, make sure the children can attend to spelling in a focussed way. Previous chapters have emphasised the importance of ensuring that transcriptional strains do not stifle the children's compositional powers and it is, of course, just as important that children should be similarly free to attend to transcription. So discrete sessions are needed and so is an emphasis on attending to spelling in the editing stage. Occasionally a compositional context, rewriting a known story for example, will be fairly undemanding so a focus on spelling would be manageable and appropriate.

The fourth 'rule', and it is one that holds good for all aspects of presentation, is to do with context and the importance of reminding children that such work belongs to the realms of real life reading and writing. A cautionary tale comes from my early years of teaching when I worked hard to teach my eight year olds how to do cursive (joined up) writing. After a few weeks I realised that they were doing beautiful joined up writing in their handwriting books but nowhere else! The Literacy Hour, where work is grounded in shared texts, provides an excellent framework for keeping the children's eyes on context. Take a Year 2 teacher looking at the prefix 'un-' (Word level work, Year 2.2). She spends a fifteen minute whole-class slot on a piece of shared writing about an unhappy caterpillar and goes on to make a shared list of words with the children that take the 'un-' prefix. Later in the week this is revisited with the whole class, whose attention is drawn to this page in an enlarged version of *Six Dinner Sid* by Inga Moore: 'Unlike Aristotle Street, the people who lived in Pythagoras Place talked with their neighbours'. In independent group work the children work as 'word detectives' hunting out their own examples from a range of carefully chosen picture books and pages from comics and newspapers.

What?

The National Curriculum provides a list of what should be covered in Key Stages One and Two. You will probably be using the Word level work from the *NLS* framework as a structure for progression and it lays down exactly what you should be teaching and when. This section is to help you with ideas for the actual teaching.

The *NLS* does not include a Literacy Hour for the nursery but the *Desirable Learning Outcomes* stress the importance of rhymes and names and also the use of 'pictures, symbols, familiar words and letters'. You will need to look at Chapter 3, which describes particular routines such as dictated writing and shared writing that are most important for the early years. As children make early moves into writing teachers can begin to alert their attention to letters and words. The child's own name is a significant first source of information as is the environmental print he or she sees all around on packets, signs and notices. You need to ensure that your classroom is print-rich and exploits these early understandings by providing many opportunities for children to write (e.g. shopping lists pads in the role-play area, a noticeboard with examples of environmental print, children's names prominently displayed). Shared reading and shared writing provide ideal contexts for making links with letters that the children already know. As well as a rich range of literature and non-fiction you will need a selection of alphabet friezes and books and lots of rhyming texts. As you know from an earlier section in this chapter, there is important work to be done with such texts in the early years in developing phonemic awareness. We cannot start work on individual sounds if children are unable to single them out, and plenty of reading aloud as well as sharing nursery rhymes and finger rhymes will all feed such awareness.

The suggestions that follow are grouped around broad strands from the *NLS*. Some are particularly appropriate for the early years or later Key Stage Two work but many can be differentiated according to the needs and abilities of the children you work with. There is not room in a book like this to include detailed activities so some books are recommended that have full details of useful activities. They are all included in the booklist at the end of the chapter. You will also find Sue Palmer's *From A–Z* an invaluable source of information about the origins and complexities of the letters of the alphabet. It was published weekly in the *Times Educational Supplement* (1997–8) and it would be well worth seeking out past copies.

Alphabetic knowledge

- Have a good range of books and friezes (on the wall and on the tables).
- Sing and chant the alphabet.
- Make alphabets for younger classses.
- Make address/phone books.
- Have lots of different materials for making letters with (paint, sand, magnetic letters, plasticine, felt tips, crayons).
- Play 'I spy. . . .'

Names

- Have name cards for the children.
- Spot letters, letter strings from names in other words (especially environmental print with young children).
- Make books featuring children's names.
- Play with names e.g. make up alliterative phrases.

See Washtell and Laycock (1996) for many ideas using children's names and the alphabet.

Rhyme and word play

- Make regular use of songs and finger rhymes.
- Read nursery rhymes and rhyming texts aloud regularly.
- Collect jingles.
- Encourage children to participate in shared reading of rhyming texts.
- Make lists of words that rhyme from texts you have read together.
- Make up games e.g. rhyming snap.
- Make up alliterative phrases and sentences. Spot examples of alliteration in poetry.
- Older children can look for rhyming patterns in poetry and try writing their own e.g. limericks.

See Washtell and Laycock's (*op. cit.*) section on 'Rhyme and Alliteration' for more games.

Homonyms and homophones

- Build on word play ideas to look at words that are spelled the same but mean different things (homonyms), as in 'Follow my lead, drop the lead, use unleaded petrol', and to look at words like 'bare' and 'bear' that sound the same but are spelled differently (homophones).
- Make books to illustrate the differences.

Onset and rime

- See 'Rhyme' above.
- Read books like *Mig the Pig* (Colin and Jacqui Hawkins) where the changing onsets are made very clear through the use of split pages; go on to make one like it using a different rime.
- Set up activities where children can physically change the onsets of words e.g. with cards, magnetic letters.

Learning words

Children need to develop a sight vocabulary of known words and the *NLS* contains lists of words to be learnt from Reception through to Year 5. Try to vary the ways in which you teach these:

- Point them out in shared reading and writing.
- Use 'look-cover-write-check'.
- Play games e.g. snap.
- Focus on one a day ('word of the day').
- Include them in wordsearches and crossword puzzles.
- Group them e.g. by initial sounds, meaning, letter strings. . . .
- Have children keep personal lists ('my spelling targets for the week').
- Make a shared list with the children of ways of remembering spelling (see list under Spelling Strategies above).
- Find out about software that allows children to practise spelling e.g. the interactive *Fisher-Price A-B-Cs* (by ABLAC on CD for WINPC) for young children, which has

musical rhyming and spelling games; *I Hate Spelling* (Dorling Kindersley) for older children has an intergalactic setting in which children travel to different planets to meet spelling challenges.

- Use talking books software on the computer, e.g. Talking stories *Oxford Reading Tree* is now available in this form. You can highlight particular words by clicking on them.

See Hackman and Trickett (1996) for a useful selection of activities on 'How to Learn a Spelling'.

Developing visual strategies

As well as learning whole words children need to develop visual (or graphic) strategies to remember strings of letters. All of the suggestions above will help this as will the following:

- Play 'Shannon's Game', which is like 'Hangman' but you have to guess the letters in order, which encourages the children to predict common letter strings.
- Teach and encourage the use of analogy e.g. by collecting words that share the same rimes such as '-ight', or '-an'.

Work on phonemes, blends and digraphs

- Find examples in shared reading and writing.
- Find examples in the children's names.
- Make up tongue twisters and alliterative sentences.
- Make word wheels.
- Make a *br*ick wall of words that start with the 'br' blend, a *tr*ain of 'tr' words and so on!
- Make a display of objects and pictures starting with the phoneme/blend/digraph.
- Make a shared list of words that children can add to during the week.
- Play 'I spy'; children could make 'I spy . . .' quiz cards for a particular sound e.g. '. . . something beginning with "ch"'.

Work on roots, prefixes and suffixes

- Look at roots of words and see how many different ways you can make them 'grow' using prefixes and suffixes e.g. 'eat': 'uneatable', 'eating', 'eater'.
- Use shared reading and shared writing to demonstrate fixed inflectional endings such as '-ed' and '-s'.
- Make shared lists of prefixes, find out where they come from (Latin or Greek) and what they mean e.g. 'photo-' is from Greek and means 'light'; 'bi-' is from Latin and means 'two'. See Pratley (1988) for useful lists.
- Collect verbs that take the regular '-ed' suffix and sort them according to the different sounds these endings make e.g. ripped, pinned, rushed, robbed, saved, plodded, laughed. . . .
- Make collections of words that share prefixes e.g. 'un-'. Take a theme such as 'giants' and use this as a starting point for drawing and/or writing about the Unwell, Unhappy, Unwise, Unreasonable . . . Giant.

- Investigate the ways in which derivational suffixes change the word class e.g. 'eat', a verb, becomes a noun with the addition of '-er': 'eater'.
- Use an IT package like *Fun School Spelling* (by Europress for DOS and on CD for PC). This focusses on prefixes and suffixes (as well as homophones) and is set in a circus.

Using dictionaries and word banks

- Have a good range of dictionaries in all classes.
- Use word level slots or short class/group sessions to demonstrate dictionary skills.
- Turn class word banks into mini-dictionaries. A word bank for your work about Victorian England can become a Victorian dictionary.
- Multimedia information sources now include dictionaries e.g. *Oxford Compendium* (OUP on CD for WINPC) includes the *Concise Oxford Dictionary* and *Oxford Thesaurus*.

See Hackman and Trickett (*op. cit.*) for an excellent range of dictionary activities.

Finding out about words: etymology, loan words and word families

- Encourage curiosity in words.
- Show children how to use an etymological dictionary (which will always list the abbreviations used e.g. L for Latin).
- Look at lists of loan words and research their origins e.g. judo (Japanese), zebra (Bantu), pyjamas (Persian), yacht (Dutch).
- Categorise words into families e.g. centigrade, centurion, centipede. . . .
- Make collections of acronyms (LASER etc.) and neologisms.
- Find out about the stories of words e.g. the silent 'b' in 'debt' came about in the sixteenth century when scholars wanted to show off their knowledge of Latin, so changed 'dette' (Middle English word) to 'debt' to show they knew it came from the Latin 'debitum'. Look for other examples of these in the section on 'Curiosities' in Laycock and Washtell (1996).

Independence and risk taking

While some children will happily 'have-a-go' at spellings others are much more reluctant. We have already talked about the importance of focussing on the bits of the word that the child has got right. Here are a few more ways to boost confidence:

- Give them 'have a go' books or encourage them to have-a-go on a separate piece of paper.
- Encourage them to write as much or as little of the word as they can even if this is just the first letter.
- Suggest they draw a 'magic line' where the spelling should be if they are really stuck (but be careful about this one; some children latch on to this too readily and their writing becomes a mass of magic lines!)
- Make sure that you demonstrate that crossing out is acceptable when drafting; do this ostentatiously during shared writing.

- Encourage the child to work on a word processer right from the start (it is not just for the final product!) and to use the spell-check function. Alert children to the aspects they do not check e.g. grammar, so that 'She gave them there dinner' would not be picked up because 'there' is correctly spelt.
- Use a spell-check package like *Co-Writer* (Don Johnston for Mac) which allows you to type a few letters and then shows possible words which the child can click on to choose.
- Use a hand held spell-checker where the child types in a word and it gives alternatives.
- Use speech support on the computer; most new PCs come with this option whereby each word is spoken as the child writes (or it can be set to read back after each sentence or as you prompt).
- Discuss spelling strategies with the whole class thus reminding them of the many different ways they can tackle spellings (see section above on Spelling Strategies).
- Make class lists of relevant spellings for a topic e.g. on a word mobile.
- Make a class list of different ways the children can find out how to spell a word without asking you e.g. from notices on the wall, from books, from a word bank, from a writing partner. . . .

Glossary

ACRONYM:	a word made up from the first letters of words e.g. LASER (Light Amplification by the Stimulated Emission of Radiation)
AFFIX:	prefixes and suffixes joined to base words e.g. 'un-' and '-ing'
ALLITERATION:	where words start with the same phoneme e.g. 'six sizzling sausages'
BLEND:	sounds which run together e.g. 'br', 'spl'
BOUND MORPHEME:	a morpheme (see below) that has to be attached to another morpheme in order to make sense e.g. 's' on the end of 'dogs'
DERIVATIONAL AFFIXES:	create new words e.g. 'teach' changes meaning with the addition of the suffix '-er' to become 'teacher'
DIGRAPH:	two letters which make one speech sound e.g. 'ch', 'ai'
ETYMOLOGY:	the history of words
FREE MORPHEME:	a morpheme (see below) which can stand on its own e.g. 'dog'
GRAPHEME:	the smallest unit of sound represented as a written symbol. The twenty-six letters of the alphabet are graphemes and so are groups of letters which emerge as one sound e.g. 'ow' in 'hollow'
HOMONYMS:	words that are spelt the same but mean something different e.g. 'font' (as in church and PC)
HOMOPHONE:	words that sound the same but mean different things e.g. 'bear/bare'
INFLECTIONAL AFFIXES:	suffixes which mark grammatical contrasts. In English these are to mark plurals, possession, subject–verb

	agreement and comparatives and superlatives
LOAN WORD:	words that have been 'borrowed' from other languages e.g. 'bungalow' from Hindi
MORPHEME:	units of meaning that cannot be broken down any more e.g. dog
MORPHOLOGY:	the study of the structure of words
NEOLOGISM:	new word
ORTHOGRAPHY:	a language's writing system (i.e. letters, spelling and punctuation conventions)
ONSET AND RIME:	'onset' is the consonant or cluster of consonants at the beginning of a word or syllable which precede the vowel, e.g. 'str(-ing)'. 'Rime' is the rest of the word or syllable, including the vowel, which enables the word to rhyme with other words e.g. '(str-)ing'
PHONEME:	the smallest unit of sound that can be spoken or heard such as 'b' in 'bat'. Meaning changes with the replacement of the phoneme e.g. 'cat' or 'bag'. Over forty-four vowel and consonant sounds have been identified in English
PHONEMIC AWARENESS:	is the ability to detect phoneme distinctions
PHONOLOGICAL AWARENESS:	the ability to hear and detect difference in sounds
PREFIX:	an affix at the beginning of a word, e.g. '*dis*appear' or '*un*pleasant'
ROOT:	the 'base' or 'stem' of a word to which prefixes and suffixes can be added e.g. 'teach'
SUFFIX:	an affix at the end of a word, e.g. 'count*ed*', 'help*ful*'
SYLLABLE:	segment of a word that always includes a vowel (with 'y' counting as a vowel in this case)

Further reading

Hackman, S. and Trickett, L. (1996) *Spelling 9–13*. London: Hodder and Stoughton.

Laycock, L. and Washtell, A. (1996) *Curriculum Bank Key Stage Two Spelling and Phonics*. Leamington Spa: Scholastic.

Ramsden, M. (1993) *Rescuing Spelling*. Devon: Southgate Publishers.

Torbe, M. (1995) *Teaching and Learning Spelling*, 3rd edn. East Grinstead: Ward Lock.

Washtell, A. and Laycock, L. (1996) *Curriculum Bank Key Stage One Spelling and Phonics*. Leamington Spa: Scholastic.

PUNCTUATION

. . . it breaks it up, otherwise it would just make a lot of nonsense. . . .

. . . annoying little things that make you stop writing. . . .

(Two six year olds on punctuation)

Despite the second child's misgivings in the above, punctuation is crucial to coherence, clarity and meaning in writing but it is a more elusive and low profile aspect of presentation than spelling or handwriting. Why is this? At a glance it seems to be rather straightforward, with a relatively small number of punctuation 'marks' whose functions seem quite clear (see the Glossary at the end of this section to check those functions). Its elusiveness is partly because there is relatively little research evidence about punctuation compared to the wealth that has been amassed about other areas of writing. It is also due to the fact that understanding punctuation is part of a larger web of complex understanding that the child has to grapple with: namely the differences between spoken and written language and, in particular, the concept of a sentence.

The inclusion of punctuation in a chapter on transcription is itself questionable because of the central role it plays in determining meaning. Michael Rosen (1995) gives us these examples which children enjoy, and which make a telling point:

> The butler stood by the door and called the guests' names.
> The butler stood by the door and called the guests names. (p. 40)

Indeed, the first version of the English *National Curriculum* included punctuation in Attainment Target 1 (Composition) because 'it helps the reader to identify the units of structure and meaning that the writer has constructed' (Cox, 1991; p. 148). Interestingly, and maybe reinforcing the earlier point about scant research in this area, this is the only reference to punctuation in Cox's chapter on Writing. For this book we have chosen to discuss punctuation alongside spelling and handwriting as we believe it is more easily understood and tackled as part of the secretarial aspect of writing. As the well crafted little story in Figure 5.11 by a six year old shows, an insistence on correct punctuation

The Moon Who Lost His Shine
One day Sophie
was walking in the woods
when darkness fell,
so she started off home.
When she was nearly home
she saw the moon.
Sophie said 'Mr Moon,
what are you looking for?'
He said he was looking for
his shine.
So she said she would help him
find it and the moon said 'Yes
please' so she did. Then Sophie
said 'Mr Moon, Mr Moon, I've found
your shine, come and look.'
She had found it in a pile of logs.
The moon was delighted and said
'Thank you for helping' and Sophie
said 'That's all right'
and went back
to tell her mum all about it.
(corrected version)

Figure 5.11

in a first go at a piece of writing could be as stifling to the child's compositional confidence and opportunity as could a similar insistence on correct spellings (as we discussed in the section on Spelling).

In this section I will look at what punctuation does, at some of the problems it presents and at what is known about how children learn to punctuate. The final section is on teaching punctuation.

What is punctuation?

Martens and Goodman (1996) give us the following definition:

> Punctuation is the conventionalised means by which an author shares with a reader necessary information about meaning or language structure not contained in the words of the text. Grammatical divisions such as sentences, clauses, phrases and words, along with marks signifying meaning, such as exclamations, support, clarify and enhance written messages for the reader.
> (p. 37)

In spoken language we use a range of linguistic and paralinguistic devices to make our meaning clear. These devices include intonation, stress, gestures and pauses. None of these is available to the writer who has to turn to the orthographic device of punctuation to do this work. If you think of the way your voice rises at the end of a question you can see how a question mark provides a written equivalent. Now try the same with exclamation marks: 'Get me some honey or I'll hit you with my bommy knocker!' shouts the giant in *The Hungry Giant* (Story Chest, 1980). Take away the exclamation mark and see how much calmer his demand becomes. You could even try replacing the exclamation mark with a question mark (which may feel clumsy but bear with the activity) and see what a difference that makes to the way you read the piece. So question marks and exclamation marks contribute towards stress (or emphasis) and intonation.

Other punctuation marks act as boundary markers. They differentiate between different structural units: phrases, clauses, sentences and direct speech. Look at the sentence I have just written and note the colon between the main clause and the list (which is a phrase), the comma separating elements of the phrase, and the full stop marking the end of the sentence. If you feel unsure about these conventions the best way to reinforce understanding (and this works very well with children) is to seek out examples in literature.

Punctuation problems.

So far so good, but it is not all quite so easy. For a start, the rules of punctuation are a convention and not very stable; they have been and continue to be subject to much change. Secondly, hearing and identifying the structural units mentioned above is not something children find easy. I will take each of these problems in turn.

Changing rules

Like spelling, the conventions surrounding punctuation have changed over time. Crystal (1995) tells us that the very earliest texts did not even have gaps between words, let alone any punctuation marks. It seems that punctuation was first introduced as a way of indicating how the text should be read aloud, as reading aloud – 'oratory' as it was called – used to be a high status activity. In fact Parkes (in Hall and Robinson, 1996) found that it was the reader who put in the punctuation in Roman times. In England, it was not until the seventeenth century that punctuation began to be used to mark grammatical distinctions. The notoriously problematic and misused apostrophe for possession was not introduced until the second half of the seventeenth century and speech marks were not used for direct speech until the eighteenth. Commas and full stops are two of the oldest marks, whereas the question mark is a relative newcomer on the scene (Clark, 1996). Some marks are no longer used: for instance, Crystal describes an ivy leaf shaped 'hedera' which was used in Anglo-Saxon writing to mark the end of a piece of writing.

Caxton's printing press (1476) was a major stabiliser for different aspects of language, particularly for the development of a standard English (the East Midlands dialect) and spelling. For spelling, further consolidation came in 1755 with the first dictionary. Therefore, although the printing press did bring some stability to punctuation conventions, they have not been subject to the same degree of standardisation as spelling and remain quite flexible. As I write, there are renewed calls for the apostrophe that marks possession (see above) to be abolished.

Authors seem to vary in the status they give to punctuation. Crystal tells us that, although Charles Dickens was punctilious in his use of punctuation, William Wordsworth left his to the publisher. The authors of *Writing Under Control* had no such options! The publisher's notes on the final presentation tell us that 'Although the book will be professionally copy-edited and proofread, the author is responsible for correct spelling and punctuation' (Fulton, 1998; p. 1).

Older children will enjoy knowing something of punctuation's evolution and it will help them think about the functions of contemporary punctuation marks. You will find ideas below which will encourage this.

Spoken and written language

We look now at punctuation's function as a boundary marker in writing. One major difference between speech and writing is that speech occurs in 'utterances' – chains of clauses which are rarely completely formed sentences. Typically these clauses will be joined by conjunctions such as 'and' and there will be many pauses, false starts and 'vague completers' (i.e. implied appeals to the listener such as 'isn't it/innit' and 'you know'). Look back at Chapter 2 for more detail about these differences.

Writing, on the other hand, uses the sentence as its basic unit so a prerequisite for placing full stops, question marks and exclamation marks appropriately is an understanding of what a sentence is. The *NLS* says that 'a sentence is a unit of written language which makes sense on its own'. The authors go on to identify four types of sentence, to describe the punctuation required and to say that most sentences will have a subject and predicate (see next paragraph). As teachers, it is important that we have a clear definition but, as you will appreciate, explaining this to children is not so straightforward.

Hall (Hall and Robinson, 1996) gives us a clear overview of some of the difficulties children can experience with grasping such definitions of a sentence. It is important to say here that Hall was writing before the advent of the *NLS*, so was not criticising its definition, but his comments do cast critical light on it. He points out that young children find grammatical definitions abstract and hard; we ourselves may grapple with the notions of 'subject' and 'predicate' with varying degrees of confidence so it is harder still for a child. He also suggests that the idea of a sentence 'making sense' is problematic: 'Does a word have complete sense? Does a sentence have complete sense if it is part of a paragraph, or a chapter or a book?' (Hall and Robinson, 1996; p. 15). You will see children in school finding their own ways of tackling these difficulties, maybe by imposing physical boundaries and putting capital letters at the beginning of a line and full stops at the end, regardless of meaning. One such example is illustrated in Figure 5.12.

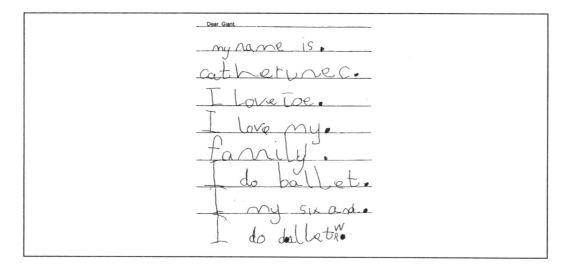

Figure 5.12

All of this is not intended to deter you from helping children to understand sentences. There are practical ideas included in the final section which are informed by what we now go on to look at: the experiences and understanding that children do bring to learning about sentences and using punctuation.

How do children learn to punctuate?

Despite the lack of research in this area it is possible to draw on our understandings about children's moves into writing in order to illuminate some key aspects of learning about punctuation.

Learning about sentences

Unless children have experienced some kind of language delay, they generally come to school as competent speakers of their mother tongue. This means that they have a lot of implicit knowledge about how language works syntactically (such as in what kind of order words occur) but they will not be so attuned to the concept of a sentence which belongs to written language. You will remember from Chapter 2 that Kress (1982) showed how children's difficulties in learning about sentences are best understood when seen as part of the child's moves from spoken to written mode.

Many children will have made a start in securing understanding of written language, particularly if they have been read to from an early age. Studies of children's early reading behaviour (Holdaway, 1979) and of their dictated stories (Fox, 1993, and see Chapter 3 of this book) show children using structures from written language in oral retellings. As a child retells a story or dictates one, he or she will pause or add appropriate emphasis in ways which suggest an understanding, again implicit, of the sentence as a unit. Here is a dictated story by a four year old; obviously you cannot hear him tell it but if you read it aloud you will see how sure his understanding is of sentence boundaries and other punctuation conventions such as exclamation marks. Included in Matthew's story is a favourite video character, Captain Planet, and two characters, Mr Wiggle and Mr Waggle, who featured in a story he was told at school:

> Captain Planet was flying about looking for his friend the Planeteer. He saw Mr Wiggle and Mr Waggle. He said, 'You can play in my spaceship but you don't touch any of the buttons.' But the naughty pair touched a big red button which sent them flying off to the moon in one hour. Captain Planet flew to the moon and told them not to press any more buttons. The next day they went exploring and Captain Planet got them some flying pizzas. Captain Planet said 'You can fly home now and tell your friend Matthew what happened.' When they woke up they thought it was a dream but then they heard 'Look out!' (child asked for this to be written 'big') and Captain Planet swooped down from the ceiling and said 'Do you think it was a dream? No such thing as dreams.'

Now look back at Figure 5.11, the six year old's story about *How the Moon Lost His Shine*. If you read it through, you will find that it is syntactically very accurate and that you can infer the punctuation quite easily even though she has only used a full stop twice. Take the opening: 'One day Sophie was walking in the woods when darkness fell so she hurried off home'. This complex sentence includes: a main clause, 'One day Sophie was walking in the woods'; a subordinate clause, 'when darkness fell'; and a coordinated clause, 'so she hurried home'. Although the child has not used any punctuation she has organised the units on separate lines showing an awareness of them as different from each other. If you look at the rest of the story you will see that, although she does not make consistent use of such a device throughout, she does seem to be making some use of layout as a substitute for punctuation.

It is reassuring then to have such evidence which suggests children can develop an implicit early understanding about sentences. The stronger that children's implicit understandings about language are, the more potential there is for making their knowledge explicit, and it is for this reason that we include reading aloud, shared reading and shared writing in the section on teaching punctuation. The latter two routines can both provide opportunities to teach about specific aspects of punctuation, but joint readings and composition will also develop more explicit understanding about sentence structure. The practice of encouraging children to read their written work aloud works in the same way, encouraging them to draw on implicit knowledge about word order and the 'flow' of language.

Learning about punctuation: the marks and the system

Environmental print is a rich source of information about writing, and it is not hard to find examples of question marks and exclamation marks scattered liberally around the supermarket and video screen. However, some aspects of it are more visible and accessible than others. Exclamation marks and question marks are high profile and easily spotted, so children can relish detecting and using them. The same cannot really be said for apostrophes, especially as there are so many public misuses of them – I recently spotted 'lunche's' on a menu board. All of this has implications when we come to think about the order in which we should teach punctuation marks. I address this in the teaching section below.

   Research that we look at in other parts of this book has shown the discoveries very young children make about the form and functions of writing; examples of children's early writing attempts will often include punctuation marks. Figure 5.13 is a three year old's list dotted with letter-like and punctuation-like marks.

   Look back to Figure 5.4 to remind yourself of Kelly's heavily drawn full stop between the first and second words. You will remember that she was beginning to make word boundaries so was probably using the full stop to reinforce the space. In Figure 5.14 the child (Reception) told her teacher that 'It's the story of knock, knock, who's there?'

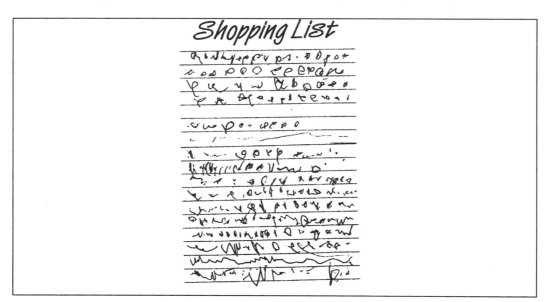

Figure 5.13

   A Shared Reading session using an enlarged text had been used to point out question marks, which the child has clearly taken on board. So she incorporates them into the text, but not with a clear understanding of the function of the symbols themselves. Her use of a range of different writing-like symbols is typical of the earliest stages of writing. Such symbols may include up and down lines (as in Figure 5.1), letters, numbers, letter-like shapes, letters from different orthographies (see Figure 5.3), mathematical symbols and punctuation marks. A key element of early writing is the

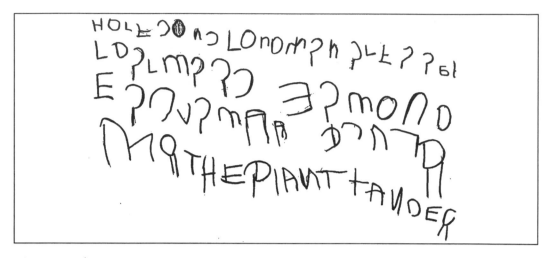

Figure 5.14

enjoyment children experience in playing with and organising these different symbols. There is something graphically satisfying about punctuation and you will all have favourite examples of children of all ages relishing the use (and often overuse) of a newly learned mark. Figure 5.15 is a Year 2 child making accurate and clearly enjoyed use of the full stop.

There is, of course, an important difference between using a symbol and understanding its significance; as children's understanding develops, so their use of symbols becomes increasingly differentiated. Martens and Goodman (in Hall and Robinson, 1996) looked at young children's use of punctuation and found examples of children working with punctuation in specific ways that reflect the nature of the system. Some examples show invented punctuation symbols which added meaning to writing and they give a wonderful example of an eight year old's invention of a 'sadlamation' mark:

> I've invented a new punctuation mark. A mark for something sad. It is used in a sentence like this. I had a dog. It died (mark inserted – a v with a small circle attached to top of left side). It does look funny but it will get better looking soon, just like all of the others.
> (p. 38)

Figure 5.15

They also found examples of children using punctuation to mark boundaries in stretches of text, what they call 'segmentation' (p. 46).

Nigel Hall's overview of research into children's learning about punctuation suggests that it is a complex process and not 'a passive process in which children simply learn a set of rules and can then punctuate accurately' (p. 33). What the studies did show is that, in common with other aspects of the writing process, children work actively in trying to build up an understanding of the system. You only have to look back again at Ben's apostrophes (Figure 5.10) for evidence of this: he knows they are used with the letter 's' when it occurs at the end of a word but has not yet grasped the possessive principle.

A sense of audience

A factor that contributes to children's understanding of the punctuation system is their developing sense of writing for an audience, which was discussed in the chapter on composition. The point here is that, as children write for a range of audiences and purposes, they become increasingly aware of the fact that we write with a reader in mind and that punctuation is there to help that reader (and this is included in the Programme of Study for Key Stage One). This was Brian Cox's (1991) reason for including punctuation with composition, and you can see how vital it is that children keep in touch with the idea of an audience, a reader for their writing. So work about punctuation needs to be grounded in a rich writing environment. Although the *NLS* document does not use the term 'audience' until Key Stage Two in the Text level requirements, you will find many different forms of writing specified where a sense of audience is crucial. Take playing with and using lists, menus and cards (Reception), making storybooks (Year 1.1), and writing labels and diagrams (Year 1.2 and 1.3). At Key Stage Two the stipulation to write book reviews for different audiences (3.3) offers some rich possibilities: what about a review of *Snow White* for the wicked stepmother, or *Cinderella* for the ugly sisters? The stronger the sense of audience the greater the imperative to punctuate correctly.

Teaching punctuation

When?

As with spelling you will need to plan opportunities to teach punctuation both through the Literacy Hour framework (Sentence level work) through routines – and especially shared reading and writing – that may go on at other times. The *NLS* specifies that the second time slot be shared between Sentence and Word level work at Key Stage Two, but that Sentence level work at Key Stage One 'should be covered in the context of shared reading and writing'.

How?

Again, you need to look back to the 'How?' section in 'Teaching spelling'. Working positively with what the children already know and use continues to be important. As the section above on 'Changing rules' showed, punctuation, like spelling, is an area that can be a source of interest for children, so make sure you include activities (such as inventing new punctuation marks) which will foster their curiosity. Keep your work contextualised, and make sure that children really are free to focus on the particular aspect of punctuation you are trying to teach and are not trying to contend with too many different things at once. Be ready for some overgeneralisation as children start to adopt new conventions in their writing; we have seen Ben's vigorous use of apostrophes and Figure 5.16 shows an energetic overuse of exclamation marks.

Figure 5.16

This nine year old is using exclamation marks to inject expression into a lively piece, which is quite close to spoken language. You can build and refine her use of them by looking at examples in books and demonstrating their use in shared reading and writing.

What?

The *National Curriculum* gives broad guidelines for what is to be covered and the *NLS* gives a term by term progression. This starts with using capitals in Reception right through to secure use of the semi-colon in Year 6. Given what we have said about the visibility and impact of some marks – especially question and exclamation marks – you might want to explore children's understandings of these a little earlier than the *NLS* suggests (Year 1.1 and 1.2). The training materials for Sentence level work contain useful ideas for punctuation.

We have looked at the use very young children may be making of marks in their early writing and those of you working in Nurseries will need to observe such use and make sure that Shared Reading and Writing opportunities include some reference to marks that children have picked up on. Your displays of environmental print should also include examples that you can draw on.

Developing a sense of audience

- Provide writing opportunities for a range of audiences e.g. books for each other (see Chapter 4) and other classes, invitations to class assemblies, notices and so on.
- Support the above through the provision of a range of writing contexts (e.g. class cafe, shop. . . .).
- Shared reading and writing sessions where you omit punctuation will help children understand and develop a sense of audience.
- Encourage children to read their work aloud, either to themselves or to a writing partner.

Developing an understanding of sentences

- Remember that a sentence has to have a subject and a finite verb.
- Children read their work aloud (as above).
- Read aloud to the children.
- Use the children's own writing corrections – 'How did you know it wasn't right?'
- Brainstorm with the children what they think a sentence is, discuss examples of non-sentences and sentences, encourage the children to generate definitions and rules.
- Focus on a particular type of sentence e.g. interrogatives (questions), look for and make up examples.
- Focus on particular parts of speech e.g. verbs as another context for discussing sentences.
- Use shared reading and writing to talk about sentences (and see requirements for Sentence level work in the *NLS*).
- Use *Breakthrough to Literacy* sentence makers to demonstrate sentence building.

Teaching specific aspects of punctuation

- Model during shared reading/writing.
- Use the children's own work as a context.
- Punctuate text with the aspect you want to teach omitted.
- Use comic strips and speech bubbles to teach about speech marks.
- Get children to make up their own punctuation marks e.g. different 'hedera' (Crystal above) for different genres of writing, or tell them about the 'sadlamation' mark and make up marks for different emotions.
- Write style guides for younger children e.g. how to use an exclamation mark!

- Find out about the history of the mark you are teaching (e.g. question mark: 'Q' is for 'quaere', Latin word for question. Originally the whole word 'quaere' was written after a question, then shortened to 'Q', before being replaced by the mark we now use (Jarman, 1979). You may also have noticed that in Spanish the question mark is used upside down at the start of sentences as well as in its normal position at the end.
- Find examples from favourite classroom books, make lists and see if the children can start to make rules.

Play with punctuation and graphic effects

One way of helping children to understand the way punctuation functions is to 'play' with its effects.

- Exchange exclamation marks and question marks and see what the effect is on reading aloud.
- Collect examples of exaggerated and attention-grabbing uses of punctuation e.g. from advertisements and cartoon characters 'Aargh!!!'
- Use ideas from Michael Rosen's lively chapter in *Did I Hear You Write?* where he suggests ways that children can represent different effects in their writing e.g.
  A word or phrase said loudly
  A single word said very slowly, as we do when we call out for mum (!)
  (1989, p. 41)

Glossary

APOSTROPHE ('):	has two uses. It is used to show where a letter or letters have been omitted (contraction) e.g. can't, it's. With an 's' after it and placed at the end of a noun (dog's) it indicates possession; however the possessive pronoun 'its' does not follow this rule. If the noun is plural the apostrophe goes after the 's'.
BRACKETS ( ):	contain extra material within a sentence, often a complete sentence, in which case there is a full stop inside the brackets.
CAPITAL LETTERS:	are used at the beginning of sentences, for 'I' and at the start of names, places, titles, days and months.
COLON (:):	is used to precede a list, to indicate that what is to follow builds on the previous point, to precede a quote.
COMMA (,):	has many uses. Used to separate the same units in a sentence which may be words, phrases or clauses.
DASH (–):	may be used like brackets (but not for full sentences) or else preceding a final comment.
EXCLAMATION MARK (!):	is used at the end of a sentence to add force and emphasis. It is used for a range of emotions e.g. anger, happiness.
FULL STOP (.):	is used to mark the end of a sentence.
HYPHEN (-):	is used for a word break at the end of a line and for

	compounds such as 'tail-ender'.
QUESTION MARK (?):	is used at the end of a question.
SEMI-COLON (;):	is used in complex sentences to separate phrases or clauses. A bit like a long comma. Is also used to separate items being listed.
SPEECH MARKS ("" or ''):	are used to demarcate direct speech.

See *NLS* Glossary and Forrestall (1987) for more information.

FURTHER READING

Hackman, S. and Trickett, L. (1996) *Punctuation 9 – 13*. London: Hodder and Stoughton.

Hall, N. (1998) *Punctuation in the Primary School*. Reading: Reading and Language Information Centre.

HANDWRITING

At Standard 1 children should be able to form on the blackboard or slate from dictation, letters capital and small manuscript.
(1862 Standards for Writing (in Aldrich, 1982; p. 81))

The ability to write easily, quickly and legibly affects the quality of a child's written output, for difficulty with handwriting can hamper his [sic] flow of thoughts and limit his fluency.
(Bullock, 1975; p. 184)

As you will remember from earlier in this book, the teaching of writing used to consist almost entirely of handwriting exercises. The logbook from an Oxfordshire village school records younger children copying letters on to slates while the older ones were still copying but had graduated on to moral sentences to be written in copybooks (Wendlebury, Oxon – private copy). We have a richer and more balanced writing curriculum now but Bullock reminds us, nearly one hundred years later, that handwriting remains as a most important secretarial aspect of the writing process and so it does today despite the advent of word-processing.

Aims of handwriting

The *National Curriculum* requires that we teach children a legible and fluent style, and Rosemary Sassoon (1983), author of many practical and useful books about handwriting, suggests that there are three aims we should have when teaching handwriting. These are: that it is legible, that it can be speedy, and that teaching allows for development of an individual style of writing.

You might find the following activity a useful way of illuminating these aims and helping you to reflect on what is involved in handwriting. Find someone to work with and copy a passage of prose at speed for five minutes. When the time is up look at your two pieces of handwriting and discuss them using the following prompts:

- Who was able to write the fastest?
- Is the handwriting always legible?

- Were you both comfortable, i.e. could you have continued to write at speed for some time?
- Are there features which might interrupt the flow of the handwriting? Are any of these solely decorative?
- How do you both feel about your handwriting?
- Do you use different styles at times e.g. in exams, for an important letter?
- Is either of you left-handed?
- Do you have any 'favourite' writing implements?

You might also like to compare the way you positioned yourselves, held the writing implement and placed the paper. You should have found that the process of observing closely was revealing and, of course, the same holds good for our work with children. We will return to the practical implications of these observations later in the section.

Issues in the teaching of handwriting

A personal style

As I look back through examples of writing from children I taught at the very beginning of my teaching career (some twenty years back), it is their handwriting that evokes each individual child, as vividly as ever. Perhaps you have childhood memories of experimenting with different styles, implements and ink colours. Handwriting is part of our identity, our own particular hallmark, and this could be why the tradition of collecting autographs persists. You might feel that the idea of a personal style is becoming less relevant with the ever-increasing use of word processors but in word-processing personal styles also develop. We realised, as we began to edit first drafts for this book, that our colleagues had distinctive word-processing styles. They had preferred fonts, made different choices about spacing, layout and whether to print in 'draft' or not. I have childhood memories of trying to copy the handwriting style of a friend as I thought it would mean I would write with her fluency and ease. It is the notion of individuality in handwriting that brings us back to a strand that has been running through this chapter concerning the development of children's curiosity about different aspects of writing. Such curiosity can and should extend to handwriting and you will find some ideas for this in the section on teaching handwriting.

Audience and purpose: making presentational choices

Ellen and Nicola (Year 2) have been asked to make a notice for the book corner reminding the class to keep the books tidy. The notice has been planned and checked for correct spelling so now they have started on the final version. Halfway through I find Ellen standing at one end of the book corner holding the notice while Nicola is reading it from the other side of the classroom. 'We just want to make sure people can read it, miss,' they tell me.

While the notions of audience and purpose are not directly linked with the physical formation of writing, they do need reaffirming with regard to handwriting. One of the prompts in the opening activity concerned the choices we make about legibility, size, and perhaps style, which will depend on the audience and purpose of the piece of writing. You will find that the *NLS* specifies the need for 'special forms' (Year 4) of writing such as print script for posters, and the appropriate use of capitals. This ties in closely with points made in Chapter 4 regarding the different types of presentation that accompany different genres of writing. Secure understanding of both writing process and product will also enable children to make confident use of a more informal script for note taking than they would for the scribing of a favourite poem for a class anthology in their 'best' handwriting.

Cursive writing

The handwriting exercises that the children at Wendlebury Village School carried out a hundred years ago would have been written in copperplate – a cursive hand. Jarman (1979) tells us that this joined up handwriting style developed in the eighteenth century at a time when more handwriting was needed for commercial purposes and book-keeping than ever before. (Its name derives from the traditional use of a plate of copper on which a printing design would be engraved.)

After 1913, this changed, after a scholar called Edward Johnston gave a lecture to London teachers in which he suggested that children's reading would be improved by the adoption of a print script, sometimes called the 'ball and stick' method. Jarman (1979) points out that, while this did provide a clear model for reading, the 'system of building up letters from separate parts' was not conducive to a fluent and speedy hand.

There was a return to cursive writing for many children with the publication of Marian Richardson's (1935) copybooks in the 1930s. However, this return was not wholesale and different handwriting schemes have been published since then. Many of these offer a compromise between print and cursive with letters given entry and exit strokes in readiness for joining up. Recently though there has been a rather more persistent move to revive the idea of teaching children a cursive hand from the start. The argument is that it is better to start as you mean to continue, rather than learning one way and then having to relearn (as I expected my class to in the example I gave in the Spelling section). Penni Cotton (1992) cites the French model where children are taught 'l'ecriture anglaise' (cursive!) right from the start. In the nurseries all classroom labelling, letters that go home and early reading texts are in cursive script. This early exposure is reinforced outside school where many books (like Brunhoff's *Babar*), comics and displays also use cursive. Most French teachers – now and in the past – use a very similar form, so children are also likely to meet this in their parents' handwriting.

While there are issues here about the extent to which such an approach might suppress the development of an individual hand, there are also persuasive arguments about a joined up script following on more naturally from children's first writing attempts (as in Figure 5.1). It is claimed that it is easier for the children to detect separate words because they do not get muddled by spaces between letters and between words. It allows for useful links to be made with spelling, as strings of letters can be seen as a whole unit and handwriting practice can be used to reinforce such strings. Charles Cripps, in a recent lecture (date unknown), argues that such an approach sets up a motor pattern for common letter strings (e.g. -ing, -tion) and that this acts as a back-up for the visual pattern.

Some schools report enthusiastically on the benefits of this approach; others remain more sceptical, arguing that very young children's cursive attempts are poorly controlled and do not offer the clear graphic information needed in spelling. The *NLS* recommends that a print script be taught 'that will be easy to join later' (Year 1), and that joins should be taught from Year 2. Whatever the pros and cons, the outcome needs to be a system that allows the child to concentrate on composition so that letter formation does not 'hamper his flow of thoughts and limit his fluency' (Bullock, *op. cit.*).

Teaching handwriting

When?

The best time to show a child how to hold a pencil and form letters is when she or he first shows an interest in writing implements and writing. Young children are likely to hold pencils and the like long before they know about letters, so helping to establish a good grip may come before demonstrating letter formation. In the nursery, this means ensuring the provision of a range of writing materials and implements as well as the kinds of enticing writing contexts we have discussed elsewhere in this book. In addition to this, young children need the opportunities provided by activities such as modelling, cutting, sticking and lacing to develop the fine motor skills they will need for handwriting. So you will need not only to think about overall provision (see below) but also, through your observations, to be responsive to individual children's needs.

Handwriting is taught during the Word level slots during the Literacy Hour. In common with other aspects of transcription you will also want to plan other opportunities to demonstrate and reinforce work through regular routines. Shared writing is a good context to remind children about correct letter formation and, for younger children, copying and tracing activities may provide valuable extra practice (see Chapter 3). There are some television programmes that provide well contextualised opportunities for handwriting practice (e.g. *Words and Pictures, Look and Read*). Look back too at the IT suggestions in the spelling section; many of the software packages there offer spelling and handwriting practice.

How?

Again, it is important to remember that your teaching should be positive and well contextualised. Make the most of the links between spelling, phonics and handwriting and use handwriting sessions as an opportunity to reinforce and revisit spelling patterns or sound work that you have taught earlier. On the whole handwriting is best taught either as a whole-class session or during teacher focussed group work, as it is most important that you are able to observe the children so that you can check an uncomfortable grip, awkward posture or inaccurate letter formation. There will be times when children are working independently as in the earlier example of writing out a favourite poem for a class anthology. Your own handwriting is important too and you need to take every opportunity to demonstrate and model this to the children. So when you write on the board, in children's books, on worksheets and in shared writing, make sure that you are offering a consistent, good quality model of formation and presentation. If you are right-handed yourself then you need to be sensitive to the difficulties left-handers can encounter. There are recommendations for this in the checklists. There is a mail order service for left-handed equipment: the Left-Handed Company, PO Box 52, South DO, Manchester M20 2PJ.

What?

Most schools will have a policy for handwriting with regard to letter formation and when to start joining. This may be backed up by a published scheme, such as *New Nelson Handwriting* (Smith and Inglis, 1984) or the *Jarman Handwriting Scheme* (Jarman, 1982), which provide graded exercises and copybooks. If you should find yourself without such support then you will find Rosemary Sassoon's (1990) book, *Handwriting: the way to teach it*, provides useful guidance on possible models. The *NLS* offers a progression through from Reception to Year 4 with specific guidance as to when and how to start joining letters (e.g. Year 2, diagonal joins to letters without ascenders e.g. ai, ar, un). You will also need to find out if there is a school policy with regard to the use of lined or unlined paper and the types of writing implements that are available (and whether these are specific to particular age groups). See the section on Provision below for more ideas on this. As the opening activity of this section demonstrated, teaching handwriting is about more than just forming letters; the way we sit and the way we hold our pens are just two other aspects we have to think about. Checklist 1 gives some guidance on these preliminaries. The rest of this section has been organised as a series of checklists, mostly for you but there is also one for children. You will find much more detail in the books listed at the end.

CHECKLIST 1: Preliminaries

- Are the children sitting comfortably, looking ahead and leaning forward a bit?
- Are the tables or desks at a suitable height?
- Is the lighting sufficient? Left-handers will need it directed over their left shoulder.
- Is the child holding the writing implement with a comfortable and usable grip?*
- Is the paper positioned well (i.e. to the right of the body for right-handers and left for left-handers, top of page slanted to the left for right-handers, either way and at a greater angle for left-handers)?
- Can the children all see the board/copybook they are using?
- Have the children all the appropriate equipment (good quality paper and implements; you cannot form letters with care using coarse paper or soft unsharpened pencils)? Are the paper and implements the right size? Rosemary Sassoon (1983) says small children need small bits of paper so that their writing arms are neither stretched nor cramped.
- Can you observe all the children?

* The question of grip is problematic. Traditionally children were taught to use the so-called 'triangular grip' but this is not comfortable for everyone. You will need to observe the child's grip 'in use' in order to ascertain whether it is allowing for fluency and legibility. The older the child the harder it is to undo an unwieldy grip! Left-handers might find it easier if they hold the implement further up than right-handers so that they can see what they are writing. For those of you who are right-handed: the best way to understand the difficulties left-handers have is to try writing left-handed yourself. One thing you will find is that left-handers will be pushing the writing implement rather than pulling it which makes for a less smooth action and has the effect of covering (rather than uncovering) the writing.

(Many of the ideas in this section come from a SENJIT (1986) publication – see Further reading.)

CHECKLIST 2: Provision

Early years:

- Material to encourage experimentation and early mark making e.g. range of colours, sizes and types of paper, pencils, crayon, felt tips, paint, sand, plasticine.
- Examples of environmental print, frequent use of children's names (which will probably be the first word they try to write and your first opportunity to show them how to hold the implement and form the letters).

As children get older set up a handwriting area.

- Include many different writing implements. Talk about using different ones for different purposes; discuss children's favourites; try Rosemary Sassoon's idea of getting the children to try out different implements and record their findings e.g. 'the pen because it's comfortable to hold . . . and I can grip it better' (Sassoon, 1990).
- Include lined and unlined paper, line guides, rough and best paper. Again, talk with the children about the most appropriate uses for these e.g. rough for notes, unlined with line guide for writing for classroom wall.
- Include examples of different types of printing and writing e.g. James Berry and Louise Brierley's (1994) beautifully presented *Celebration Song* which has a cursively written text.
- Include different alphabet posters (English and in other scripts too e.g. Urdu, Bengali, Turkish).
- Include examples of illuminated letters which children can use to enhance presentation of special pieces of work e.g. postcards from the *Book of Kells* and from manuscripts in the British Museum, Jan Pienkowski's (1984) *Christmas*.
- Include examples of books with striking borders e.g. Antonia Barber and Nicola Bayley's (1990) *The Mousehole Cat*, Selina Hastings and Juan Wijngaard's (1985) *Sir Gawain and the Loathly Lady*.

Establishing an area like this is best done with the children, so that you can discuss the different materials and involve them in decisions about what type of implement or paper might be best suited for a particular purpose. Sassoon (1990) suggests the children could survey all the different material and draw up 'dos and don'ts for handwriting lists'. She includes some lovely drawings by children showing good and bad positioning for writing (p. 41).

CHECKLIST 3: Promoting an interest in handwriting

As well as including the range of scripts, books and letters mentioned above there are other ways of fostering children's curiosity about handwriting. You could:

- find out about the work of graphologists: people who analyse handwriting and tell us about the psychological significance of the way we form letters. Did you know, for instance, that a 'd' written with loops suggests that you are vain? (Crystal, 1995, p. 269).

- collect pictures and photos of children writing; there are many images of Victorian schools to be found;
- collect examples of handwriting from famous people; discuss autographs;
- find out about calligraphy as a craft e.g. writing implements through the ages – Jarman gives instructions as to how to make a quill pen (1979, pp. 134–5).

CHECKLIST 4: Possible problems

- Are the letters being formed correctly, completely, and consistently? (Watch out for the starting point [the top for all the letters except for 'd' and 'e' for print], stroke direction, poor joins, closure of letters such as 'a' which if not closed looks like 'ci'.)
- Are children waiting until they have completed words in cursive script before dotting the 'i' and the 'j' and crossing the 't'? In other words, check that they are not lifting their hands unnecessarily from the page.
- Is spacing between letters and words accurate?
- Are ascenders and descenders (see below) the right height and length (i.e. no more than twice the length of lower case letters)?
- Are all the downstrokes parallel?
- Is the writing too big or too small?
- Is the writing sitting on the line?
- Are bits of letters being taken out or put in (and does it matter)?

And for left-handers:

- Is the paper to the left of the child's body?
- Is s/he too close to a right-hander? Rosemary Sassoon recounts this useful little rule devised by a child for when left- and right-handers are sitting next to each other: 'Don't knock funny bones.' (1990, p. 33).
- Is the child holding the implement comfortably? (see Checklist 1 on grip)

(Some of these ideas come from John Foggin's (1992) *Real Writing* and some from Jarman.)

Finally, here is a checklist that children could use. You would probably want to adapt it depending on the age and experience of the children you work with.

CHECKLIST 5: My handwriting checklist

As you get organised to do some writing ask yourself these questions:

- Are my pens and pencils in good condition?
- Have I cleared my table so that I've got room to write?
- Am I comfortable and do I have my writing paper in a good position?

Before you start writing ask yourself these questions:

- Is there anything I need to think about to improve my handwriting?
    - the formation of letters that I find difficult to write;
    - joining my letters up;
    - making my writing sit on the line;
    - keeping my letters an even height;

– making my writing bigger or smaller;
– leaving evenly spaced gaps between my words.

● What sort of writing do I need to do?
- drafting;   – my neatest writing;
- note taking;   – word-processing.

When you finish writing ask these questions:

● Can I read my writing?
● Can other people read my writing?
● Is my writing tidy enough?
● Did I use the right kind of handwriting for the job I was doing?
● Next time, what could I improve on?

Glossary (Many of these are self-explanatory but here is a quick checklist:)

ASCENDERS:	occur in b, l, d, f, h, k, t; the part of the letter above the midpoint
CURSIVE:	joined up writing
DESCENDERS:	occur in g, j, p, q, y; the part of the letter below the line
DIAGONAL JOIN:	all letters in cursive script join to their next letter with a diagonal join except o, v, w and, in some cursives, b
ENTRY STROKE:	join or line going into the letter
EXIT STROKE:	join or line leaving the letter
HORIZONTAL JOIN:	o, v, w and, in some cursives, b join to their next letters with a horizontal join
LOWER CASE:	small letters a, b, c . . . ,
PRINT:	writing that is not joined up
UPPER CASE:	capital letters A, B, C . . . ,

Further reading

SENJIT (1986) *Ideas on Handwriting*. Available from SENJIT, University of London, Institute of Education, London WC1H 0AL.

Sassoon, R. (1990) *Handwriting: the way to teach it*. Cheltenham: Stanley Thornes.

CHAPTER 6

Monitoring and Assessing Writing

Liz Laycock

INTRODUCTION

In this chapter I shall consider what is involved in responding to, monitoring and assessing children's writing.

Children are expected to write in every area of the curriculum, so teachers have a great deal of reading and assessing to do. Sometimes the writing will be a way of assessing a child's knowledge of another subject or a way of checking the child's recall of the details of an observation or a visit. In most cases, whatever the subject, the teacher will 'mark' errors in spelling, punctuation or grammar and may make a general comment about the content or the quality of the work. The proper marking of written work is one of the ways in which those who do not see what goes on in the classroom (e.g. parents) feel they can judge a teacher's effectiveness. It is the outward and visible sign that the teacher is doing her job well.

But we need to reflect on this marking activity; it is all too often a proofreading exercise, with the teacher correcting errors of various kinds. Given the amount of time devoted to marking, we need to consider whether this is the most productive way of helping children to improve their writing skills. Not many children take our corrections so seriously that they never make errors again. Qualitative judgements such as 'good' or even 'excellent' rarely give pupils an indication of what was considered in making the judgement.

> The marking at my Primary school was not very helpful. The teachers wrote comments at the end like 'Good' or 'See me' or something like that. I used to get really annoyed when they wrote something like 'Good' and left you wondering what good really meant.
> (Year 7 pupil in *National Writing Project*, 1989)

It is most probable that the teachers' 'Good' assessments of this pupil were influenced by accurate spelling, legible handwriting and correct punctuation. When a teacher looks at a piece of writing by a child, it is easy to spot the mistakes; however competent the writer, there will generally be some spelling and punctuation errors to be corrected. Paying attention to these surface features can often prevent the teacher-reader from seeing beyond them to the content or message which was the purpose of the writing.

You may need to think in terms of 'feedback' and 'response' to writing rather than 'marking' and 'correction', and to consider the ways in which this might be achieved. One starting point might be to ensure that young writers themselves understand the criteria by which writing will be assessed. These should be made clear to pupils before they begin to write and they should understand the purpose and audience for the writing, as well as the form it should take. You might initially restrict oral or written feedback to a response to the content or to the writer's use of a particular form, offering guidance on how these could be improved, before moving on to correction of transcriptional errors. The need to separate the compositional from the transcriptional aspects of writing has been identified throughout this book, but nowhere is this more important than in the process of assessment. This is not to suggest that the mechanics of writing are unimportant; indeed, precisely because the surface features are so rapidly judged, it is vital that teachers help children to get them right. But we need to regard errors in a more positive light, seeing them as evidence of learning, as efforts to master the conventions, rather than as failure.

One of the purposes of this chapter, therefore, is to help you to get the assessment of writing under control and to offer formative assessment frameworks and procedures which allow teachers to monitor progress. Formative assessments allow you to identify the aspects of writing the pupil needs to work on and thus inform the plans you make for further teaching about writing. The teacher's cumulative record of formative assessments will provide the evidence for summative assessments, which record what the child now knows and is able to do. Summative assessments are needed at the end of a school year or Key Stage. Both types of teacher assessments are needed to provide fuller information than will be gained from tests or SAT scores alone.

You need both to observe writers at work and to look closely at samples of writing in order to analyse the children's writing strategies, their level of 'independence and confidence' as writers and their current 'knowledge and understanding' of writing. (See Barrs *et al.* (1990) for full descriptions of these 'strands of learning'.)

TEACHER ASSESSMENT OF WRITING – FORMATIVE ASSESSMENT

Observation and sampling in the early years

However young the child, it is possible, through observation of the writer at work and through analysis of the product, to identify the child's current knowledge about the purposes for writing and the kind of writing, as well as his/her hypotheses about the conventions of writing in English.

In Figure 6.1, which is by a child in a Reception class, much is visible. The inspiration for this story was a toy mouse (Freddie) in the classroom, about whom the children had composed a story through shared writing. Many then wanted to write their own stories about the mouse. Hanife told her teacher that it said:

> Freddie the mouse came out of the cupboard. Freddie the mouse came out of the door to see if it was safe. Then Freddie had a terrible fright. It was Jade's cat.

The telling of this short story shows that she has a good sense of the characteristics of the narrative form: it has a series of events leading to a climax. She was also clear about the purpose for the writing – she wanted to contribute another story about Freddie, in booklet form. The child approached the writing task with absolute confidence; she knew she could write a story and that her efforts would receive a positive response from her teacher. The picture was drawn first, on the left-hand side of the page (following the convention of many picture-story books), and represents the startled mouse meeting the cat. The writing was then fitted into the space on the right-hand

Figure 6.1

side. The first three lines were written from left to right but she then completed the page writing from right to left. The text is a mixture of real letter shapes, many of which are the letters in her name, 'Hanife', alongside letter-like shapes. There is some evidence that she is grouping letters together as in words, but there is no attempt to match the letters to the sounds of the words she is writing nor of one-to-one correspondence. The writing has a mixture of upper and lower case letters and many of them were formed in an unconventional way. (See Gentry's 'pre-communicative' stage in Chapter 5.)

Much of this information was available because the teacher had observed the writing in progress and had heard Hanife's running commentary as she completed the task. For example, Hanife had told the teacher what was in the picture and the teacher had been able to observe the shift in directionality as the child wrote. She was also able to see the way in which she formed the letters. The teacher had not intervened because she wanted to observe the child's current knowledge and understanding about writing; this was not an occasion for teaching, but for assessing before teaching. As we saw in Chapter 5, the use of known letters, most commonly from a child's name, to generate new writing is typically observed in young children's early writing and indicates that the child understands that writing is made up of letters. It is important, when samples like this are being collected, to ensure that full annotations of the context, of the child's intentions and approach, confidence and independence, are recorded, so that the evidence in the sample can be drawn upon in planning further teaching.

This teacher now knows that she will need to work on directionality of writing in English and on handwriting, as well as alphabet and letter sound knowledge. She also knows that Hanife has a basic understanding of how stories are structured which can be built on by encouraging her to write more and possibly by inviting her to dictate stories (see Chapter 3). She may also give her opportunities to experiment with other forms of writing (e.g. letters, lists).

Sampling at Year 2

Although formal assessments (e.g. SATs) are based on single pieces of writing, teacher assessments, related to the Level descriptions of the *National Curriculum*, should be made with reference to a range of samples, which reflect different purposes and genres.

In Figures 6.2 to 6.4, three pieces of writing from a Year 2 child, Martin, have been selected, though more of his output would certainly be taken into consideration by the child's teacher. The examples selected are three different genres.

The scientific investigation in Figure 6.2 approximates to what we would normally call a recount, as it is a retelling of the experiments he did. As we discussed in Chapter 4, the recount genre is one that young writers feel quite comfortable with. In fact, scientific writing such as this would typically be written as a report or a piece of procedural writing. However, unless the teacher has specified and supported the type of writing expected, it is not surprising that Martin has written a recount. Many teachers will recognise this as a transitional stage. Martin has described three different activities and has indicated this by separating the writing into three sections. His spelling is largely based upon phonic analysis of words e.g. 'lite', 'werkt', though he shows some awareness of conventional letter strings e.g. 'ends', 'line'. (See Gentry's 'phonetic stage' in Chapter 5.) He demarcates sentences with capital letters and full stops. His handwriting shows generally correct letter formation and clear ascenders and descenders.

From the evidence in this writing, the teacher can obtain a clear idea of what she needs to teach to move the child forward. For instance, he might benefit from working with a writing frame, perhaps with the use of chronological linking words (e.g. 'First . . .', 'Next . . .', 'Then . . .'). Teaching the correct spellings of words he needed to use (e.g. 'light', 'buzzer', 'battery') and the correct terminology for 'wire', 'crocodile clip', would also help.

The story in Figure 6.3, written three months later, is incomplete, but shows some features of a narrative with a sequence of events in the 'adventures of . . .' manner, on an ambitious canvas (the world!). There is not, however, a series of events moving towards a conclusion, which is fairly typical of stories when the child has not thought through ideas first and thus rambles fairly aimlessly from one event to another (see Chapter 4). His teacher had praised Martin's use of 'describing words', (though she has not given him an example of what she means), and he has the confidence to experiment with new vocabulary (e.g. 'route' spelt as 'rot').

Thursday 4th December
we made crcuits
I uesed a batry and
a lite and put the tow
ends of the lite and on the went
the lite. I uesed a batry
and a metel line and a
buset and a lite and the
buzzer werkt but the lile
dednt werk. I uesed a
batry and a buzer put
the tow ends of the buzer.
on the batry and the buzer
woukt.

battery

bulb

Figure 6.2

Since the previous sample, his spelling has progressed. There are now many high frequency words spelt correctly; some of the incorrectly spelt words show evidence of graphic awareness of conventional letter strings (e.g. 'poler') while others show spelling at the transitional stage (e.g. 'bera' for 'bear' and 'how' for 'who') with correct letters in the wrong order. He is still using phonic analysis as a strategy for tackling unknown words in some instances (e.g. 'ostralyer' for 'Australia', 'miyls' for 'miles' and 'tiyed' for 'tired'). He still spells the inflectional '-ed' ending with a 't' ('bumpt') as he did in his first

Tuesday 17th March 1998
The big big dragan and the world
Once there lived a dragon who was green with sharp spikes on his back. One day he flew away to ostrayler [Australia] with his mum. When he took the rang rot he was going to the coldest rot his mum was going home when he bumped [ed] into a big, big polar bera [bear] but lukiey [luckily] the poler bere didn't do enything to the dragon. The poler bera only said you are a beta open your mouth so I can check you. So the dragon opned [opened] his mouth so the bera cod [could] see so the beke took his head out of the dragons mouth. Then said yes you are a poler bera no I.m not ! I blow fire but you don't. So bye. Next the dragon flew ten miyts [miles] away. He got bit tiyed [tired] so he landed on afreca [Africa] for a minit [minute] but it wasnt a good rest because an elephant was chaking [shaking] the groynd.

Figure 6.3

sample – 'werkt' for 'worked'. Sentences are sometimes demarcated with a full stop, but these are not always followed by a capital letter; there is no attempt to use inverted commas to mark direct speech. He uses the apostrophe correctly in the contraction 'didn't' but not in 'wasnt'; he does not use the possessive apostrophe in 'dragons'.

Martin needs guidance to develop his control of narrative form, so a way forward might include: encouragement to plan stories, so that he has a sense of where he is proceeding; talking with him about the structure of stories and clear demonstrations of these structures. (See Chapter 4.) After praising his correct spelling, the teacher should help him to learn those words that he has misspelt but which are near to correct forms, using the 'Look, cover, write, check' routine. You will notice on Martin's writing that the teacher helped him to learn the unchanging suffix '-ed', used in words such as 'bumped' (see Chapter 5). He should be invited to edit his own writing: he could, for instance, be encouraged to underline or circle for himself those words whose spelling he feels he might need to check. As we have emphasised in other places, he will need to know how to find those words from the classroom resources. You will see that there are other errors in Martin's writing (e.g. absence of inverted commas) but you need to be aware that he will not be able to take this all on board at the same time.

The third example, Figure 6.4, was written two weeks later. It is included because it shows progress in Martin's recount writing. It is chronologically organised and the sentences are linked with appropriate connectives – 'first', 'then', 'when', and 'next'. He writes in discernible sentences although they are not all correctly punctuated (see Chapter 5). One indicator of his spelling progress is the way he has taken on his teacher's help with the '-ed' ending, making no errors with 'walked', 'looked', and 'sketched'.

Figure 6.4

These three samples of writing show progress over time in several areas: control of genre; spelling strategies; handwriting.

Using the Level descriptions

As Martin is approaching the end of Year 2/Key Stage 1, it is appropriate to look at the Level descriptions and to decide which description best fits his current achievement. These samples of writing (formative assessments), together with information gathered by his teacher during the year, will provide evidence for this summative assessment. The description for Level 2 reads:

> Pupils' writing communicates meaning in both narrative and non-narrative forms, using appropriate and interesting vocabulary, and showing some awareness of the reader. Ideas are developed in a sequence of sentences, sometimes demarcated by capital letters and full stops. Simple, monosyllabic words are usually spelt correctly, and where there are inaccuracies the alternative is phonetically plausible. In handwriting letters are accurately formed and consistent in size.

The description for Level 3 reads:

> Pupils' writing is often organised, imaginative and clear. The main features of different forms of writing are used appropriately, beginning to be adapted to different readers. Sequences of sentences extend ideas logically and words are chosen for variety and interest. The basic grammatical structure of sentences is usually correct. Spelling is usually accurate, including that of common, polysyllabic words. Punctuation to mark sentences – full stops, capital letters and question marks – is accurately used. Handwriting is joined and legible.'

Looking at these two alongside each other, it is clear that Martin has met all the criteria at Level 2 so consideration must also be given to Level 3. He is well on the way to meeting many of these criteria, certainly those which relate to the structure and content of the writing. But he does not yet meet the transcriptional criteria. We must, therefore, conclude that Level 2 is the best fit.

Another set of descriptions has been provided by the Centre for Language in Primary Education in the shape of writing scales (Barrs *et al.*, 1996). These scales map fine distinctions in children's writing achievements and may help you in amplifying the Level descriptions in the *National Curriculum*. Those teachers taking part in the piloting of the scales reported how useful they found the group moderation sessions:

> As well as providing a basis for quality assurance in assessment, moderation has other benefits. It encourages teachers to justify their judgements and to be more explicit about their approach to assessment. . . . Moderation focuses attention on the evidence for teachers' assessments, and helps to demonstrate the kinds of evidence that can be most informative in arriving at agreed judgements. In this way it can influence work on record-keeping in schools.
> (Barrs *et al.*, 1996)

Having collected samples of your children's writing you would find it valuable to discuss your own evaluations of these with a group of colleagues. You will find some guidance on this in the SCAA (1995a) publication *Consistency in Teacher Assessment: Exemplification of Standards*.

Sampling at Year 4

The samples of writing in Figures 6.5 to 6.9 cover a period of six months and a range of different kinds of writing in different curriculum areas. The writer, Jatinder, is a boy in Year 4. He was born in England and his mother is a monolingual English speaker and father speaks both English and Panjabi. Jatinder is a fluent speaker, reader and writer of English and, although a speaker of Panjabi, he is not literate in it. The pieces include a book review, some scientific writing, a letter of invitation, a story and a diary. If we view these samples as a collection made by the class teacher over time, we can see that they reflect a range of purpose and forms. In every case the teacher had given clear guidance about what was expected in the particular form and, in some cases, had provided a writing framework (not, generally, a writing frame) for guidance. Some of these samples are presented as marked by the teacher, so that her responses to the writing can be seen. In this class, books are used so that there is a blank page alongside the child's writing where the teacher can write comments, suggestions and sometimes corrections and where the child can actually redraft sections of the writing. Thus, when appropriate, the writer is given guidance about redrafting content as well as indications of where spellings need to be checked. It is obviously helpful if there is an agreed school policy on marking and correction, which children know and understand. In the absence of an existing policy, you might feel it would be worthwhile drawing up a set of marking symbols which would be explained to the children and, certainly initially, displayed in the classroom. These would need to make a distinction between the marking of transcriptional errors and ways of indicating redrafting suggestions. Once established, these could be used by children in editing their own work, and in responding to each other's work, as well as by the teacher. (See Chapter 3 on writing partnerships.)

If we look across these samples we can gather a good deal of information about Jatinder's writing.

Figure 6.5, a book review of a title selected by the writer, is succinct, includes relevant information about the book, a brief resumé and personal evaluation.

Figure 6.6 is about an experiment to find out which material best reflects light. It starts with a step by step (procedural genre) account of how they went about the experiment and then records the findings. Jatinder has clearly separated the procedure (on the left) from the findings (on the right). Vocabulary is used accurately throughout but the voice of the writer, which is appropriately impersonal in the clearly expressed instructions, takes on an understandably personal tone when describing the results.

In Figure 6.7, the address, which has been erased, was correctly laid out. This letter of invitation shows good knowledge of the letter format and tone. Writing in role to a fictitious character with an invitation to an imaginary party has provided the writer with a purposeful context and shows his command over a chronologically organised piece of writing.

In Figure 6.8, the story plan at the top allows Jatinder to decide on the setting, characters and opening line. He begins dramatically with speech without any preamble or scene setting. The content of this story derives from characteristic interests of boys of this age (see Chapters 4 and 7). The structure of the story is that of a true narrative, with a series of events, leading to a resolution (his escape), and with a most effective ending in the capture of the dog! He sustains the third person narrative throughout. There is some charac-

18.9.97 # A Book Review

~~The Aardvark Who Wasn't~~
The Author is called Jill Tomlinson.
It was a fiction book. It ~~w~~ was a ex funny
book. Ther was (were) two ardvarks. The moother
ardvark eats termits but Pim, the little
ardvark still likes milk and at the end
he is hungy at so he et some termits.
Ther was (were) not a lot of illustrations.* A teacher
read it and I listened. It was enjoy(able)ing.
I would recommend it. I would give it 5 out of
5.

Figure 6.5

1. You first get Which material best reflects ~~the~~
the equipment you   light?
need and make a
~~to~~ broken ~~curcet~~
compleate.
2. ~~Get~~ Then get
a piece of
cardbord and
make a cone
shape with a
hole in the
center.
3. Cover the
cone in tinfoil,
clear plastic,
white paper or silver
foil.
4. ~~pt~~ Put the cone
shape on the light.

We tried tinfoil
and the light
reflected ~~down~~ on
one side in a
straight line.

Somebody else
tried silver foil
and it reflated
more and brigt-
er.

Nobody tried
~~silver~~ white
paper or clear
plastic because
we thought they
would not work.

Well done, you have recorded clearly what we did,
what happened and why. I'm not sure you needed
the diagram of a complete circuit though.

Figure 6.6

Figure 6.7

terisation of the hero, Alex, in his cynicism about the letter. There is also some descriptive detail – 'wet grass', 'gigantic spaceship', 'wooden cage', 'thin stick', and 'in a dash'.

The diary entry in Figure 6.9 arose from the study of the Tudors in history. After finding out about the destruction of the Spanish Armada, the children were asked to write an account of the event in diary format. This required them to adopt a personal voice. The final version was published as a diary for display. It is written in the first person and conveys real feeling (the heat of the fire and his fear and then relief). The teacher also kept the first draft of this piece of writing in which she had responded enthusiastically to his use of similes. It is important that your collection of samples includes drafts as these can reveal the whole of the writing process and not just the final, polished version.

With these samples in front of her the teacher is in a strong position to review Jatinder's progress. As you will have seen from the comments above, this is a confident,

~~My~~ A Strange Light Plan   20.1.98

~~What sort~~ It is going to be an exciting
story.
In a new planet *It is going to take place.
The characters are a boy called Alex and
his dog called Rex.
It will be at night.
It begins with ~~Alex~~ Rex barking every
night.
It ~~was~~ is a beem of light.

_____

A Strange Light

~~Stop barking~~ Alex said to himself as his dog²
carried on barking. Then Alex sat up in bed
and ~~found~~ a letter ~~which~~ said 'Kanech Kavew
Kwooooya'. Alex was nine so he did not belive
a lot of stuff. Eventchully he looked out of the
window and saw ~~his dog~~ Rex runing around the garden.
Then he walked ~~over~~ in to the hall and went
down stairs. It was quiet now because his dog
had stopped barbking. ~~went~~ When he reched
the back door he opened it slowly then
he stepped outside on the wet grass. ~~and~~ 4 Then,
all of a sudden, a ~~a~~ beam of light lifted
Alex up in a s gigantic space ship. ~~a~~ When
he ~~was~~ arrived in the space ship he was
standing on his feet with a book in
front of him. On the front cover ~~it~~ it said
'Cooking Humans'. He opened the book and
inside it said 'boys are yumyest.' Straight
away Alex knew he had to get out of the
space ship. Alex was ~~m~~ now looking for
a way out but....
he ~~said~~ was caught by an ~~olen~~ alien. The
alien looked like an ~~a~~ Octopars with 5 eyes.
He tried to run but he ~~couldnot~~ the alien
grabed him and wouldnot let go. The alien
~~bat this but~~ him into a wooden cage.
In the morning he woke up in the cage.
Infront of him was a table ~~of~~ and on
the table was the to the ~~cave~~ cage.
He tried to reach the key but it was
too far away Then ~~b~~ he found a thin
stick on the bottom of the cage. He
vesed the stick to help him get the
key. He opened the cage and ran
in to the next room. On the floor he
saw a button. He pushed ~~the grass~~
~~He~~ In a dash he had ran in to
his bedroom. Then a stage light ~~cort~~
his eye. He ran to the window and saw
~~his~~ Rex in the air. ....

1. * STOP BARKING !.2* Re)
3.* under his pillow.

*4 Then,
(*) Maybe you could give us a bit more
here.

*5 put put

* the button and ~~landed~~
landed on

Figure 6.8

independent writer who is able to adjust his writing to different purposes and for
different genres. His teacher has already provided models and guidance for these

The Spanish Armada

It was 8th June 1588. The weather was very windy and it seemed like a tornado was going through the sea. I was in a ship called The Big Drake Sailing off the French coast near Calais. I was climbing down the rigging because I had had to untie the ropes. Suddenly I herd a big whoosh. After that came a crakerling noise. I immediately I looked forward and I saw eight fire ships sailing towards the Spanish Armada. Everything started to turn red and orange. I felt like I was going to melt. I began to panic and thought I was going to die. Then I saw the Spanish Armada scatter around us like a bunch of rats being chased by a cat. I began to feel much better. Now I am inside my house all safe and sound. I am just reminding myself what I have been through and I never want to do it again!

Figure 6.9

different genres, and, on the basis of this evidence, she is able to note areas where he needs more experience. She will be able to plan a range of opportunities to meet his needs, perhaps encouraging writing for a wider range of audiences beyond the classroom.

In all except the earliest sample, where he writes the spoken London dialect form in 'there was two . . .', 'there was not many', he uses Standard written English. He shows increasing control over complex sentence structure ('I am just reminding myself what I have been through . . .' in 6.9), figurative language ('I saw the Spanish Armada scatter around us like a bunch of rats being chased by a cat' in 6.9), the passive voice ('he was caught by an alien' in 6.8), dialogue ('"Stop barking!" Alex said . . .' in 6.8) and use of reversed word order for dramatic effect ('. . . on the floor he saw a button. . . .' in 6.8).

There is consistent evidence of Jatinder's control of the transcriptional features of writing. His spelling is generally accurate in frequently used words, both monosyllabic and polysyllabic, and he is not afraid to make attempts to spell unfamiliar words. His efforts are consistently sensible phonic attempts, (e.g. 'prervieded', 'inderpendernce', 'ervenchilly', 'cort'). He uses punctuation confidently, including the exclamation mark, and is beginning to use inverted commas for speech. He also makes use of inverted commas for quotations (He opened the book and inside it said 'Boys are yummiest' in 6.8). Only the story contains any use of paragraphing. His handwriting is legible and letters are well formed on the whole; they are joined some of the time, though he often prints when he is writing quickly. Some explicit teaching about the conventions of punctuation, about visual spelling patterns (e.g. for words with 'e' which might sound like 'er' in the child's particular speech patterns, such as 'eventually', 'even', 'parents') might be needed. He might also be given time to practise joined handwriting in order to develop a secure cursive script which will promote speed even in first drafts (see Chapter 5).

Jatinder is in Year 4 and therefore not at the end of a Key Stage, so the use of Level descriptions to make summative statements about his writing is not required. We can say, though, that given the supportive, explicit teaching about writing he is currently receiving, he is well on the way to achieving at least Level 4 by the end of Year 6.

With samples such as these the child and parents, as well as any teacher, are able to review progress. The child can highlight those aspects of writing with which he is pleased and where he feels he has made progress, as well as reflect upon and perhaps set himself targets for areas he needs to work on. The child and his teacher can usefully think about how he feels he might best be helped and a record of such a conference can be made so that the child can look back and see where he has developed. When you first undertake a writing conference with a child, it is useful to have an aide-mémoire of topics for discussion. This might include asking the child to select a piece of writing from any area of the curriculum with which he is particularly pleased. You might then ask why he thinks this is a good piece, what was done well, as well as which kinds of writing he enjoys. Sometimes a child will tell you about writing enjoyed at home; if writing outside school is not mentioned, you could prompt with a comment about your own personal writing (letters, stories, poetry . . .), or a question. It is quite revealing to ask how the child thinks you could help to improve his writing – you will often find out, from the response to this question, what the child considers to be important in writing.

Many LEAs and individual schools have developed frameworks for annotating samples of children's writing, for noting observations of children at work and for recording discussions with children. One of the most helpful is that provided by the *Primary Language Record* (Barrs *et al.*, 1988) or the *Primary Learning Record* (Hester *et al.*, 1993), developed by the Centre for Language in Primary Education (CLPE), from which many other records have been derived. The *PLR* is currently being revised to provide greater differentiation in the foci at different stages (Early Years, Key Stage One and Key Stage Two).

Another record which has recently been developed by Croydon LEA, *Writing Development; a Framework* (Graham, 1995), focusses on common development patterns and provides a checklist of statements about children working within each National Curriculum Level, from 1 to 5. This framework makes a clear distinction between compositional and transcriptional features of writing and teachers highlight statements as they are observed in examples of a child's writing. The compilers point out that the unhighlighted statements provide guidance for teachers about the experiences and teaching which will need to be incorporated into future planning.

STANDARD ASSESSMENT TASKS FOR WRITING (SATS)

Key Stage One

The assessment of writing at the end of Key Stage One is carried out by means of a writing *task* rather than a test. The children's writing should be 'developed from reading a book on either of the (SAT) booklists or from a book related to other work in the classroom' (QCA, 1997). The teacher selects and reads the book and decides on the kind of writing most appropriate to its content. This might be a personal account, informative writing, instructions, letters, personal response/review or writing which extends or adapts ideas or language patterns from the original book. 'The writing task should generally be completed in one session which should not last more than an hour.' The children's writing must be independent and 'assessed without further refinement, because redrafting is not part of this assessment'.

This task, apart from the exclusion of the drafting stage, would not be very different from much normal classroom writing, for many children. Different starting points from different books can be used, selected by the teacher, so that a child is carrying out the sort of writing with which he or she is most confident. The session is introduced in a similar way to ordinary writing sessions, with discussion and guidance from the teacher to help the children think through what they will write, though no specific word lists, story openings or models are given. The children must then write independently, using whatever resources they normally use (e.g. wordbooks, dictionaries, general wall displays), but teachers must not give assistance. The assessment of the completed writing is carried out by the teacher, and the *English Tasks Teacher's Handbook* (QCA, 1997) gives detailed guidance about this, including a set of examples for different levels. Simple assessment sheets (one per child), with prompts, are provided for teachers to record the evidence gleaned from the writing sample.

At this stage the only aspect of writing to be formally tested is spelling. For 1997–8, the use of the spelling test for children assessed by teachers as being Level 1 was optional, but 'Children whose teacher assessment in Writing is Level 2 or above, or who achieve Level 2 or Level 3 in the writing task, must be entered for the test.' (QCA/DfEE, 1997)

The test is contained in a booklet divided into two parts: Part 1 contains 10 picture-based single word spelling questions and Part 2 is a continuous passage containing 20 target words. There is no time limit to the test and it is possible to take a break part way through. Each child has a copy of the booklet, and the words to be written are dictated by the teacher. Children are reminded that they should have a go at all the words, even if they can write only the beginning or part of a word. It is important that they are confident enough to do this because correct initial consonants gain one mark and a correctly spelt word a second mark (two for each word is possible). Most of the words are those frequently used by children, though there are some less usual ones, e.g. 'seat', 'pavement', and 'luckily'.

Key Stage Two

Writing test

This is a timed test: 15 minutes for planning and 45 minutes to write. Children are given a booklet with a choice of different kinds of writing and planning sheets for these. In 1998, children had to choose from four given titles/genres: 'Read all about it!' – an interview; 'The School Trip' – a newsletter; 'You're in Charge' and 'Changes' – short stories. As an introduction to the session, the teacher reads through this planning booklet with the children, pointing out the requirements for each piece and the prompts given. The prompts include reminders about both the structure and the layout of the different kinds of writing; for the stories, writers are reminded of the need to identify characters, setting and events and, in the case of the information writing, a clearly defined purpose and audience is described. Children use the initial booklet to plan their writing, which must be done individually without any discussion with other children. A separate booklet is provided for the actual writing.

There is no invitation or opportunity to redraft, though there might be time for editing. The fact that the test requires 'one-off' pieces of writing does not mean that all of the children's classroom writing should be produced in this way. The routines of planning and drafting will certainly help children in the test situation, though, in the weeks before the SAT, children should also have had some practice in planning and writing to time.

These tests are marked by external markers who are given fairly tight criteria to work to. These criteria are available for teachers but not 'until all of the Key Stage 2 tests have taken place'! The writing is marked with reference to 'two broad categories: Purpose and Organisation, and Grammar (sub-divided into Punctuation and Style)'.

Spelling and Handwriting are not part of the criteria (see separate tests). In the mark scheme booklet, sample scripts from different levels have been annotated, with comments under the two headings, to show how the criteria should be interpreted in context.

Spelling and handwriting test

This is a separate test which takes ten minutes to administer. The teacher reads the passage (in 1998, about 'Taking the Train') and the children write the words into the gaps in their version of the text, in the Spelling and Handwriting booklet. Following the spelling test, children must then copy out, in their neatest handwriting, the passage which is printed in the booklet. The teacher reads out the text before the children begin to write. Both of these tests are also marked externally and marking criteria, with exemplars, are provided.

Instructions for all of these tests include a note reminding teachers that EAL pupils are not permitted to use bilingual dictionaries and that translations should not be given in any of the English test materials. Many pupils who are at an early stage in developing fluency in English may, therefore, find the test activities rather stressful and you should be aware of the effect of the tests on the confidence of such children.

For children who are judged to be working at National Curriculum Level 6, there is an additional, 60 minute, extension test of writing which includes an extended answer for the final question. In 1997 the writing was in the form of a letter to a newspaper. This is the writing assessment and it is marked using the same criteria (Purpose and Organisation, and Grammar) as the main writing test, though with the addition of Presentational (spelling and handwriting) criteria.

The content of the Key Stage Two SATs changes from year to year, but the basic format and the aspects of writing being tested have remained, with very little variation, for three years. These formal tests must be taken by children throughout the country on the same dates in May and an examination timetable is set in advance. Schools must not open the packs of test papers until the day of the test. There is no doubt that children will need some preparation for these tests, especially if they have been used to working collaboratively and discussing ongoing writing with others. As has been already said, there is no need to change normal working practices in the classroom.

It is the 'whole writing experience' which is the source of the detailed information needed to monitor each child's development and to plan appropriate teaching. Some of the writing experiences can be incorporated into Literacy Hour activities, but remember that you will need to make provision for more extended writing and for writing in the non-literary genres associated with other curriculum areas. If you look back at the writing samples from Jatinder you will see that some of these arise from science and history and that the characteristics of the genres required needed to be taught in the context of those subjects. The writing element of the English curriculum crosses curriculum boundaries and you will need to be aware of this when you monitor and assess children's writing output. If you have collected samples of writing and have annotated them throughout the year, not only will you be able to focus your planning more precisely, but you will also have all the information you need to make summative Teacher Assessments of the children's progress at the end of the year.

Further Reading

Barrs, M. and Johnston, G. (1993) *Record-Keeping in the Primary School.* London: Hodder and Stoughton

Sainsbury, M. (1996) *Tracking Significant Achievement in Primary English.* London: Hodder and Stoughton.

CHAPTER 7

Meeting Individual Needs

Judith Graham

> We clearly need a body of research that addresses the writing problems faced by individual learners in today's classrooms. There is scant research focused on the children who struggle in writing classrooms across the grades; on linguistically diverse writers; on children, who despite all efforts, do not grasp sound-symbol relations; on children who are disinterested* in writing; and on special needs children who are mainstreamed into writing classrooms.
> (Dahl and Farnan, 1998; pp. 35–6)

* In the UK, we would use 'uninterested'.

In this final chapter, we think about children as individuals who often demonstrate very different achievements in writing, not only in what they choose to write about but also in the levels of attainment that they reach. In most classes, among the children whose progress is sure and steady, there will be some children who write willingly enough but with many errors, some who tend to write about the same topic again and again, some who write at length but with no commitment, some who claim that they hate writing and do the bare minimum or refuse to write at all. In the first set of examples that follow, all these behaviours will be discussed and suggestions for help offered. The 'linguistically diverse' writers of whom Dahl and Farnan speak are then discussed and finally the writing differences between boys and girls.

CHILDREN WHO WRITE WILLINGLY ENOUGH BUT WITH MANY ERRORS

Eight year old Bethany wrote this piece voluntarily and without help. I present it here with transcription aspects tidied up. I suggest you do not look at the original just yet.

> Once upon a time, there was a little boy. He was just at the edge of the cliff. He fell. I ran to the phone box and phoned the ambulance. The ambulance came as quick as possible. They took him to the hospital as fast as the ambulance went. He broke his head and he died.
>
> His mum and dad came to the hospital. They were very upset. They was crying all year because he was only four years old. His brothers and sisters were very upset as well.
>
> All of the family came to the funeral. All grandmas and all the grandpas came. They all sang to him.
>
> The next day was his birthday. They all made a cake. It was a chocolate one. And then they put some balloons up. They put lots of seats on the table. All the brothers and sisters sat down. And his mum and dad sat down. And they prayed to him. They had a birthday party.
>
> After that, they went out. They went to the cinema and had a good time and when they came back they thought about brother.

At this point you will probably feel that Bethany has done quite well to sustain a piece of writing of this length and that, on the whole, she has shaped the piece well and remained on topic, albeit swinging rather giddily between death and life. You will be impressed by her hold on family behaviour at crisis times and also by her characters' resilience. You may be wondering to what extent it reflects both fantasy and real elements in her life. On a second reading, you may note some confusion with genres: after a 'once upon a time' opening, we do not expect a disaster account and a first person narrator. You may also think that a child who demonstrates competence with two subordinate clauses, adverbial clauses of reason and of time, could be expected to write with even more complex sentences. But there is lots to commend in this piece and to discuss with its author.

In Figure 7.1 you will see that Bethany's work has been presented with a lot of 'surface noise'. So much in fact, that, in a busy classroom, there would not be time to 'translate' the piece as I have done in order to reveal its characteristics. You can see at a glance that Bethany has transcription problems of every kind. Spelling is phonically logical in some words ('wus a pnr' – once upon a; 'hosbtol' – hospital; 'sisds' – sisters; 'aftdr' – after) but not in others ('hudt' – head; 'ckee' – cake; 'fock' – thought). Her handwriting makes her spelling appear even more alarming: her representation of words such as 'party' and 'after', which appear to be spelled 'pute' and 'uftdr', are probably spelled 'pate' and 'aftdr' but, because she does not close her lower case letter 'a', the words have an apparent arbitrariness about them. Several other letters are wrongly or tentatively formed and re-formed so that we have to work hard to select the correct letter from a graphic arrangement that suggests many. Full stops are mostly in place but they are not followed by capital letters. Capitals, however, appear wrongly in 'MuM' and 'DaD' and 'Ran'. The piece is not paragraphed.

What is a busy teacher to do? In the long run, the most efficient and the most helpful action you can take is to devote time to this one piece and do a full analysis of it. You will then have so much information that you can work on with your pupil that the time will seem a small price to pay for the quality and efficacy of the help which you will then be in a position to offer. You will not of course be able or want to work on more than one or two noted items at any one time; there is ample evidence that children such as Bethany can become quickly discouraged or resistant if you point out too many errors. You will also want to decide an order of priority based on what Bethany can understand and what will make the greatest impact on the writing. Half a term spent working with her on the following should mean that the next piece you sit down to analyse has far fewer transcription errors. Some of Bethany's errors will be shared by others in the class and can be addressed during the Literacy Hour.

Presentation

- Encourage crossing out of a word and re-writing rather than the modifying and over-writing we see throughout this piece.
- Move her into cursive script (signs are there already) and encourage her to keep her pen on the page to form letters correctly.
- Word-process to give her work a professional appearance.

wus a ponr a tum thery was
a little boy he was chuc at
the ech of the chlif. he fel
I Ran to the foon box and
foond the ablissn the ablissn
cham is thck as posbl. they tod
him to hosbtol is fusd as the
ablissn went. he brooct his hudt
and he dud. his mum a DaD chem
to the hosbtol. they wor vere
upset they wos chrun owt yir
becks he was onke for yise old.
they his brufis and sisds wor vere
upset is wel. owl of the fumle
chem to the funeowl. owl gramus
and owl the grenDaDS chem.
they owl sugr to him. the nexs
day was his brday. they owl med
a chee. it was a chokl one.
and then they poot sum badons.
up up. they poot lots of sets on the
tebbl. owl the bruss and sidis sat
dan. and his Mum and DaD sat
dan. and they prayd to him. they
had a brfda pute. ufedr that they
went owt. they went to the senumrs
and had a good turm and wen thay
came back they fock abont brufr.

　　　✗　　　The End

Figure 7.1

Spelling

● Starting with words like 'was' (which she spells both correctly and incorrectly in this piece) get certain words into her sight vocabulary. Show her how well that works for her with words like 'the' which she always spells correctly.

- Get her to see that 'y' represents the sound at the end of many words ('only', 'very') where she is using an 'e'.
- Help her with the 'ck' digraph, at least at the start of words, where it is never found. Her spellings of 'cliff', 'came', 'crying', 'because', 'took' and 'broke' are all affected by an overgeneralised use of 'ck'.
- Teach her that the inflectional suffix '-ed' is unchanging so it is very easy to get right in words like 'phoned', 'prayed'. Similarly, knowing that the inflectional '-s' is for plurals will help her to avoid mistakes like 'yise' for 'years'. (See Chapters 5 and 6.)
- See if she can detect syllables and, if she can, teach her that every syllable has at least one vowel. She will then have more chance of getting 'brothers', 'sisters' and 'family' right.
- Help her to stretch out words orally so that she can hear their component phonemes. This may be useful in conjunction with seeing the words in print also – notice that her spelling of several words such as 'gramus' (grandmas) and 'funeowl' (funeral) probably indicates good aural ability but no visual fine-tuning.

Punctuation

- Show Bethany how good she is at putting in full stops and tell her you know that she can do it always. Teach her to follow full stops with capitals.

In addition to the above, you will have noticed that Bethany finds it very difficult to represent vowel sounds correctly: 'wor' – were; 'owl' – all; 'yir' – year; 'brufis' – brothers; 'fumle' – family. This is Bethany's biggest challenge. Achieve success in other areas first and then see if work on onset and rime will help her see the regular patterns: 'others, smothers, mothers, brothers'. (See Chapter 5.) All the time, she will need to be reading and/or listening to you reading while she has her eyes on the text, so that her visual strategies develop to complement her aural discrimination.

Before I leave Bethany, it needs to be stressed that her willingness to write readily and at length is at risk unless your approach is sensitive. I have detailed the work that needs to be done on transcription aspects; I am not suggesting that there are no improvements to be made on the compositional side but, in relative terms, she is not doing too badly there so keep her morale high while also making the odd suggestion – such as a bit more pre-planning and revision so that the story-telling opening goes and the 'I' in the story is clarified or excised. Publish her work so that she can see the correct forms of her words and so that she feels her work reaches a wider audience.

CHILDREN WHO TEND TO WRITE ABOUT THE SAME TOPIC AGAIN AND AGAIN

Week 1 Some tanks can go into the water. They can still have the guns.
Week 2 The tank has two little guns and the little guns fire little bullets.
Week 3 Some tanks have little guns and big guns.
Week 4 The big tank is a 101 Fighter Fox.
(Kevin, age 6)

There are plenty of explanations for children who tend to write on the same topic over and over again. They may have had success once and be living in hope that the experience will be repeated. They may be extremely interested in the topic and not realise that their rehearsal of content does not enchant everybody. They may feel that their position in the class as authority on a topic may be at risk if they move away from it. Importantly, they may be using the period of writing always about the same things to make progress in some of the transcription sides of writing. Above all, they may be nervous of branching out into new areas. Security in what they know may be important and you will want to respect this.

If you are sure that the writing is not showing any signs of growth for the child, in any area, then consider one or more of the following:

- Increase the amount of time which the child spends writing. We all tend to go round in circles if we do not write frequently enough.
- Get the child to read out work to the class more often in order to elicit peer reaction. The class comments may shift the child into providing more interesting detail and eventually into new areas.
- Publish the child's work so that an end product marks visible achievement and, with luck, a sense of closure.
- Increase the child's exposure to a range of genres and provide new audiences. Kevin could be encouraged to make a picture book for younger children in which a disaster occurs to those guns under water.
- Support moves into new areas: with reading aloud, visits, TV programmes, the offer of taking dictation, writing frames, etc.
- Model (in shared writing sessions) how you move on to new topics when you think it is time.
- Congratulate him when he does branch out. (See further comments on this in Boys and Girls below.)

CHILDREN WHO WRITE AT LENGTH BUT WITH NO COMMITMENT

> Once upon a time there were some teddy bears. They went to school. They had the register and then they took out their books. One bear did not listen. He got sent to the corner and had to do sums all the time and then it was home time. When they got home they set off on a boat to go to France and had something to eat (etc.)
> (Lucy, age 8)

Commitment, or lack of it, is difficult to demonstrate simply by presenting an end product. The above child continued this piece for several more pages, adding incidents competently but in an unplanned and disaffected way. There are many such children who settle down immediately to write on given writing tasks and produce the required amount with little fuss and acceptable accuracy but do not seem to care about planning, revising, redrafting, publishing or feedback. It seems as if they are privileging the length of the piece above content; this may be a reflection of teachers' messages about minimum length requirements regardless of genre.

Lucy does not of course keep us awake at night in the way that Bethany does. But there is much that we can do to improve her writing and increase engagement. Try some or all of the following:

- Increase the sense of audience. Children who write only for the teacher are in danger of losing a critical, reflective stance towards their writing. This writer is clearly imitating a young children's book; given the opportunity to read to a real audience of small children, she would probably have planned more carefully, added dialogue and ensured a sense of a significant problem and a final resolution and evaluation.

- Ask the child about the details that are so carefully avoided here. In talk, and when she realised that there was genuine interest in her ideas, this child said that it was because the bear had been so excited about France that he could not concentrate at school and that, because he had been fiddling with the teacher's things, he had had a smack. Many children just do not realise how such detail, far from holding up the story, gives the piece voice and particularity.

- Get writing partnerships going in the classroom (see Chapter 3). Other children will increase Lucy's ambition to improve her writing and getting closer to others' writing will make Lucy care about the community of writers to which she belongs.

- Encourage Lucy to write voluntarily rather than at prescribed times, so that she does not fall into the mechanical writing that she produces so easily on request. Inviting writing areas can be a great incentive (see Chapters 3 and 5).

- Find out what Lucy would really like to write about. Donald Graves' (1983) suggestions for notebooks for individual writing topics are useful.

CHILDREN WHO CLAIM THAT THEY HATE WRITING AND DO THE BARE MINIMUM OR NOTHING AT ALL

Once upon a time there was a dinosaur and
(Neil, age 7)

Most scraps of writing like this end up in the wastepaper basket, thrown there after 30 minutes of a wasted lesson by an angry or despondent child or by the teacher when she retrieves the tightly screwed up ball from under the desk. It is a situation familiar to most teachers and very worrying. Usually these children will add a word or two if you are sitting beside them but once you leave then they will dry up again. The reasons for this behaviour fall into two main categories: anxiety about getting it wrong and a shortage of ideas. The suggestions below deal with both these categories:

- Anxieties about getting it wrong are nearly always to do with transcription elements – letter formation, crossings-out, spelling errors, punctuation omissions. Occasionally they are about content; for instance, if the child is to write a non-fiction piece and you have expressly forbidden copying from information sources and the child does not know how to complete the task in any other way. If you can get the child dictating to you, not only has he the opportunity to witness innumerable lessons on how to form letters, punctuate, paragraph and spell but also more of his story is preserved, so that his morale is raised and at some point he may be willing to take over the writing.

- Reassure the child that many excellent writers leave transcription aspects until after they have got their content down. Have an editing table in your classroom where the piece can go for tidying up by you or appropriate others.

- When the child is stuck on the spelling of a word, suggest that they 'have-a-go' in a notebook kept for that purpose, find a source for the word in the classroom or write it for them. (See Chapter 5.) It is important that you do not give the impression that writing equals spelling, so keep this bit 'light'.

- Try to give more prior support before you expect writing. Make sure that the topic has been discussed, that a structure is identified and, on some occasions, supplied, that key words are written up to jog memories, that the audience for the piece is identified. (See Chapter 4.)
- Make it quite clear that this is not the final draft, but still ensure that materials which the child is working with are not too scruffy. Many a child will write more readily when they are given your special sharp pencil or a fine felt tip. (See Chapter 5.)
- If children lose heart, suggest that they look at other writers' work to see if they can find inspiration or solutions. Suggest that they go on to some different work and let them return to the piece another day. (Real writers do this.)
- Keep a record of the topics that are of interest to the child so that you can suggest an area when inspiration is short. Remind children of pieces that they have written which you have enjoyed.
- Provide small enticements to write; post-it pads and novelty notebooks may lure the most diffident of writers.
- Allow time away from writing to decorate or illustrate the piece. Time spent on, for instance, illuminating the first letter, is often used fruitfully to muse on how the text could develop.
- Use the word processor both as an incentive and also as a reward for getting on with the work – but do not disrupt the classroom routines you have established for the equipment. (See Chapter 3.)
- Keep a file (with an index) of all writing done, however short, so that the child can see the progress being made.

You will see that there are common themes that keep occurring in these suggestions for children with writing difficulties or reluctance. In truth, what is good practice for all your class is good practice for these children too. Obviously there would be no need, for instance, to scribe for a fluent writer but that child, in her time, may have benefited enormously from such a practice. Regard your inexperienced writer as just that – inexperienced – and do not attribute errors to carelessness nor reluctance to laziness. It is mostly more complicated than that. One of the advantages of a Literacy Hour – in the sense of a predictable classroom routine that will provide structure and regularity – is that it is the less secure children in your classroom who will appreciate the consistency and continuity. Try to provide as much writing time as possible for your children with difficulties, especially of extended pieces. You will also want to encourage writing at home as much as you can (see Chapter 3).

CHILDREN LEARNING TO WRITE IN ENGLISH AS AN ADDITIONAL LANGUAGE

Before we look at writing with children whose first language is not English, it is important to remind ourselves of what we know in three areas:

1. What do we know about how human beings learn language?
2. What do we know about how human beings learn a second or subsequent language?
3. What do teachers do to give EAL children access to good teaching?

What do we know about how human beings learn language?

We know that we learn language through being surrounded by people using the target language in meaningful circumstances. Because of the nature of children's early lives, some of the language they hear, especially that which is directed at them, is repeated, stressed and simplified. We know that children's language learning involves listening, thinking, playing and adjusting. We know that children experiment with sounds and use intonation 'tunes' to make themselves understood. We know that it is helpful if children are allowed to initiate topics of interest. We know that it is important that people respond to children's approximations and treat them as meaningful. We know that correction of the forms of the language is largely ineffectual in the early stages. Children will go on saying, 'I wented' and 'Mummy goed' and even 'I caughted it' for a long time despite well meaning correction.

What do we know about how human beings learn a second or subsequent language?

Children learning English as an additional language need very similar conditions to those in which they learned their first language. They similarly need models, meaningful circumstances, some stressing, repetition and simplification, time to listen and no pressure to speak until ready, freedom to make mistakes, a chance to choose the topic, a chance to play.

What do teachers do to give EAL children access to good teaching?

In the classroom, the teacher will have to respect the EAL child's early silence and receive responses in non-verbal forms initially. The meaningful classroom which she has created for all children will serve her EAL children well. She will offer planned and structured group work where groups are, ideally, mixed race, gender, ability and language; she will recognise the power and learning potential in narrative, song, drama and story-telling; she will read from fiction and non-fiction texts to her class; she will organise computer time, visits, taped texts in the listening corner and numerous practical activities. She will want to pursue parental involvement and to ensure that the school adheres to its anti-racist policies. In addition, the teacher will check for anglocentric content in her resources and activities, put up multilingual displays and bring texts in other languages into the classroom.

The teacher will need to make some moves more deliberately and be more focussed in her language strategies when she is teaching EAL children and thus she will encourage mother-tongue use, knowing as she does that progress there will be reflected in increased competence in English (see Chapter 2). She will use bilingual helpers to help her make fair assessments, of oral as well as written work, and she will team-teach with them where possible, especially in the Literacy Hour. She will ask for their help or advice in preparing big books and school-made cassettes in two or more languages. As far as writing is concerned, she will encourage children to write in all their languages, use older children to scribe for younger children in their first languages, taking dictation herself and inviting parents to participate in writing activities with their children. She will have overlay keyboards and computer programmes such as *All Write* (ILECC, 1988). Posters around the school and letters home will be in translated form as far as possible, not just to convey contents but also to signal respect for the languages in the community.

Classroom examples

The following examples will illustrate ways of working with EAL children in the writing classroom in which it can be seen that the teachers and schools involved understand the importance of the areas discussed above.

Early Years and Key Stage One

A Year 1 class has been looking at scripts in various languages. All around the room are examples of Chinese, Bengali and Urdu, brought in by the teacher, the children and parents. After a visit to a Chinese restaurant in Soho (where some of the Chinese children were able to show off their reading of the menu), the Chinese script was very high profile for a while. Nil's writing, in Figure 7.2, is in both Bengali and Chinese.

Figure 7.2

The next piece, Figure 7.3, by Yesmin is interesting as the gap between her competence in Bengali and English is apparent in the tentative copying of her name in the less familiar script used for English (scribed initially by the teacher). Direction and sequence of letters are a problem for her at this stage but her interest in different scripts ensured that she took notice as her teacher scribed for her and for the class.

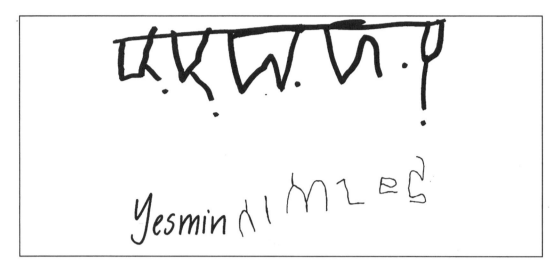

Figure 7.3

Shared writing produced a set of instructions and drawings for how to use chopsticks and then captions for a set of photographs of the visit to Soho Chinatown (later made into a spiral-bound class book). All the time, there was lots of emergent writing in several scripts to which the teacher responded positively. The piece by Mahbuba, Figure 7.4, was not 'translated' by the child, who was still at the silent stage, but the teacher pointed out features of various scripts, much to the child's pleasure.

Figure 7.4

In this class, children chose which language they were going to write in and responded to the hospitality their teacher gave to their languages. The teacher dated, glossed and kept all work, even 'unfinished' pieces, and was able at the end of the children's first full year in school to share the progress made, both with them and with their parents. Anxieties, expressed by some parents that progress in English would suffer if first languages were encouraged, were mostly allayed in the light of the children's achievements.

Key Stage Two

In a Year 4 class, the teacher had been sharing traditional tales from several cultures with the class. *Bimwili and the Zimwi* (Aardema and Medhaugh) had been shared several times and a whole-class drama had developed (everybody became the drum, the seagull, the waves of the sea as required). Many of the children could retell the story in story-telling sessions and all the class could sing Bimwili's plaintive ditties. The class was bonded to this story forever it seemed. Many children wrote alternative endings, extra scenes, interior monologues but, for the three EAL children whose work is reproduced in Figure 7.5, the fluency they found came from a retelling. Not reproduced here is the fine picture they drew while they were planning the retelling.

Figure 7.5

There are errors of course – the one the teacher chose to work on was the '-ed' suffix, which helped sort out 'dropt' and 'ript', where the children have not yet internalised the regular third person past tense and are representing what they can hear. (Bethany has a similar problem.) But remarkable is the control over the main shape of the story, the introduction of dialogue (albeit without punctuation) and a command over English sentence structure that is closing in on the standard within the class as a whole. Children experimenting with new constructions in writing – such as the sentence beginning 'When her mother' – tend to make errors which they cannot pick up with proofreading. They need increased familiarity with the constructions and careful teacher support in pointing them out.

Reading and writing connections

This work with traditional tales depends on the teacher being enthusiastic about reading aloud and building up the secondary world which children can then revisit any time in their heads. Re-readings allow deeper meanings to evolve and the texts assume greater and greater importance to children. In addition, with the all-important exposure to the unchanging text, children get some of that same repetition and intonation 'tune' that supported their entry into spoken language. It is very clear that children learning English can hold many of the structures and much of the vocabulary of English when the structures and words are charged with memorable and symbolic meaning. Many a child's writing discloses the rhythms, vocabulary and cadences of an original text, such as 'he begged and begged and begged but no . . .' or 'Now it was not long before . . .' or 'Suddenly a voice was heard' or 'Where there is water, there are fish and where there are fish, there are fishermen'. It reminds us how closely tied reading is to children's writing development. EAL children need to be read to as much as you can manage.

BOYS AND GIRLS

In a chapter on individual needs, the heading 'Boys and girls' may be rather surprising. It probably suggests a mass divided broadly into two roughly equal parts rather than the specialised few whom we have been considering up to this point under the headings of 'children with difficulties' or 'EAL children'. But as groups, boys and girls left to their own devices tend to restrict their writing choices and depend much on peer approval and what it is considered fashionable. It is important to discuss the pertinent issues here.

Social conditioning

Because subtle and not so subtle assumptions about sex-roles are everywhere in society, including in our classrooms, and because these assumptions affect life experiences, we as teachers have a certain responsibility to try to counteract some of these limiting expectations. The differing social conditioning of boys and girls means that by the time children are in nursery school, a noticeable preference to play outside, to play with large construction toys and to draw and fantasise about large, often destructive, items is evident in the small boys. The girls will more commonly be drawn to activities at tables, be found in elaborate games of domestic play in play corners and be involved in talk with the adults around. In terms of their story reading and television watching and video game playing, noticeable general differences are observable, with girls and boys demonstrating clear gendered differences from an early age.

Classroom action

Teachers have tried to make changes in some of the following ways:

- by monitoring and guiding the activities that children choose in free time. Parents and helpers can be useful allies to get the girls to play with Lego and to get the boys into the role-play area.
- by discussing issues with children, e.g. their toys, colours of clothes for babies, advertisements, suitable presents for relations, etc.;
- by sharing books which foreground some of the issues, e.g. *Piggybook* (Browne), *Jump* (Magorian and Ormerod);
- by helping girls and boys to role-play characters of the opposite sex;
- by checking that all children read fiction and non-fiction;
- by deciding what to do about certain traditional fairy stories and comics;
- by checking that both sexes are represented as central characters in the fiction shared;
- by checking illustrations of roles taken by male and female;
- by checking that authors are men and women;
- by inviting non-stereotypical visitors e.g. female doctors and male nurses into the classroom for children to talk to. A male embroiderer invited into school worked a miracle for boys' needlework. Another class had a visitor (female) who had survived the Japanese earthquake (two days stuck in a lift) and although her account was not overly heroic, her bravery left a marked impression, particularly on the boys of the class.

Writing and gender

Particularly in writing, teachers have often felt that gender differences are most marked. Boys and girls do very different things in their writing.

Early Years and Key Stage One

Under various action-packed pictures, these captions (transcription aspects are tidied up) appeared in the first school work produced by four year old Ben:

This is a dinosaur and a volcano erupted and some anti-aircraft guns and some people killed the dinosaur.

This is a sports car and an interceptor was in the sky.

This is a swimming pool and Aaron went off the diving board and it was the top board.

This is a golden eagle and it is on the mountains.

This is a dynamite and a aeroplane fired a long rope and a circle of bombs made the dynamite go off.

This is a lighthouse and a robber stole a ship and it was tied on a stick and the robber tried to cut the rope but he couldn't.

This is a lunar module and it is taking off and two space men are climbing into the lunar module.

This is a submarine and a shark came along.

Here are four year old Claire's captions under her drawings:

I went to the seaside and it wasn't all in sand. It was in stones.

The princess is mending the giant's socks and she is sitting on a chair.

My brother Mark when he had a wobbly tooth it went down the plug hole.

We had a game of getting married and Natalie sprinkled (sbrigcwld!) the poppy petals on my head for confetti.

Gillian read me a story and then I went to sleep with my knees curled up.

Both sets of captions have imaginative and linguistic strengths but Claire's focus on family, friends, the personal and the domestic (even in the giant's home) is in marked contrast to Ben's inventory of all the most extreme, violent, powerful and, one has to say it, phallic things he writes about.

Key Stage Two

Do matters change after the children have been in school for three or four years? It will probably not be difficult for you to guess which of the two recounts below was written by a girl and which by a boy. Each child was exactly the same age (7 years, 11 months).

> We went to Seven Sisters Rocks to-day and we crossed the Suspension Bridge. We had to walk a long way and we saw an elm tree and it had Dutch elm disease. We climbed a steep rock. Then we got to the first one of the Seven Sisters rocks. We had a look down from the top of the rock and it was a brilliant view. We went to King Arthur's cave and it was full of rubbish. We had a snack. We had an apple and cucumber and raisins. Some people were rolling rocks down the drop. On the way back, we saw an ants nest and someone threw a stone on the nest and all the ants came out to repair it.

> On Wednesday, Polly came to stay the night and we played with our little pets, the guinea pigs. We had Snowdrop which was an albino. It was all white with red beady eyes and Joseph, he had all sorts of colours just like a multi-coloured coat. And that's why we called him Joseph. Rachel tied her green bracelet into the cage and the baby guinea pigs jumped through. Polly liked Snowdrop best because it was an albino. Jessica, Polly's sister, was allergic to them so she could not hold them. Then we gave them a lesson to jump through the hoop. It was Snowdrop's turn first. He did it nicely. Then it was Joseph's turn. He did it a bit wrong. At the end of the lesson, we had our tea.

The first text confirms what is generally felt about boys' writing: that it roams further afield than that of girls; that it includes more action; and that it contains more evidence of interest in boyish behaviour. In this case, the boys who threw rocks over the edge and who stone the ants' nest receive no disapproval. (It is possible that the writer joined in with the activities.) It is probable that the audience the writer was hoping to interest in his piece was his own circle of boys who were on the outing and peer approval is no small consideration as we have indicated earlier.

The second piece conforms to a general expectation of a piece from a girl of this age: it is home-focussed and concerned with the intimate goings-on of life with family, friends and domestic animals. It is focussed throughout on one topic and presents a story which is carefully shaped and cosy in its tone. The audience for this piece was ostensibly the girl's teacher; however, there is some indication that the extra information (how Joseph came by his name, where Jessica fits in) is considerately provided not only for her teacher but also perhaps for some wider, unknown audience.

A better future?

After one has read several pieces of writing which appear to confirm these general characteristics of the content and tone of girls' and boys' writing one does doubt whether the efforts teachers make such as those outlined above can make much difference. Certainly we need to investigate and research even more those classrooms where boys and girls are confounding our expectations. There is promising evidence, for instance, that the recent understandings of how to scaffold non-fiction writing with 'writing frames' is giving a boost to girls' writing in that area.

In looking through the notebooks of writing from several boys and girls (from which the above examples have been taken), I am struck by the fact that, although the trend in boys and girls is clearly gender-marked, in all the notebooks there were atypical examples of writing – far fewer in number but clearly there nevertheless. Thus Ben drew a careful picture of his garden, captioned:

Daddy mended the fence and we had a pic-nic

and Claire had a dramatic picture, captioned:

A man and a boy are out in the frost with a dog and the dog fell in some ice and drowned.

At age eight, there was a comparable sprinkling of writing where one would be hard-pressed to guess whether the author was male or female. If teachers notice, commend, share and publish these unrepresentative pieces, children may begin to shift in their understanding of the range they can attempt. The impact of what children have read to them is also significant as is the gender of the reader. What is popular reading in the classroom is influential also. Eve Bearne (1998) knows of Year 6 boys who write romances while Judy Blume is the class cult reading, and girls who are laying out their non-fiction writing with large exploded inserts and pull-out maps.

It is true also that boys are likely to read and write more and differently when they have male examples at school and at home. As most primary school teachers are female and as we cannot arrange for a male in every home, this becomes a tall order, but where schools have, for instance, invited male authors into school, writing's profile has been helpfully increased. Michael Rosen's school visits, where he shares his non-stereotypical poetry with children, have done their part in this long haul towards a widening of what girls and boys see themselves able to write.

CHILDREN WHOSE WRITTEN WORK SHOWS GRAMMATICAL ERRORS

There have been several instances in the examples of writing that we have used throughout this book of children who import features of their spoken language into their writing. For all children, spoken language acquisition is ahead of written competence as they have obviously not had the same exposure to written language, which is nearly always in Standard English. The most obvious errors in this respect are those of non-agreement of subject and verb; thus in Bethany's writing, we find, 'the parents *was* crying' (Figure 7.1), in Jatinder's writing, 'there *was* two ardvarks' and 'there *was* not a lot of illustrations' (Figure 6.5). Other errors appear in writing in places where we would not notice them in speech. You see an example of this in 'the shop keeper who owned the shop did not know that there was one everyone wanted the christmas tree but it was too expensive' (Figure 5.8). In this section I look at key issues of grammar teaching, part of Language Study in the *National Curriculum*.

What can be taught?

As we saw in Chapter 2 there has been considerable debate about how and what should be taught explicitly as far as grammar is concerned We will not rehearse those arguments here but will remind you that the *NLS* provides a framework for contextualised grammar teaching (Sentence level work). The difficulty will be to find ways round the abstractions involved in teaching some aspects. If you cannot explain a rule in straightforward language and in a way that children can take on then it is probably wiser to put your time and effort into lots of examples of the rule in practice, so that children can generate their own understandings and definitions. It is also important to remember that many children have already acquired Standard English and use it without error in their writing, so some in your class will bring a great deal of implicit understanding to the teaching you do.

The importance of reading to children and of children reading in the development of their acquisition of written Standard English cannot be emphasised enough.

When to deal with grammatical errors that appear in individual writing

If children are well practised in reading their work aloud, either to themselves or a writing partner, then they are more than likely to pick up some of their grammatical errors. When 7 year old Tony read out his story and came to the sentence 'That night the rabbit's mum comed to the lion's den . . .' he said straightaway 'That doesn't sound right' and changed it to the past tense of the irregular verb 'to come'. If a child's writing reaches the editing table with grammatical errors still present, individual help will need to be given by the teacher and final marking left in her hands so that no work reaches a wider public with non-standard slips in place. At this final stage the child will be far more interested in the lessons to be learned than if you interrupt the flow of composition at the start of the process. As this book has consistently maintained, it is most important that children know when it is most profitable to give their attention to the various different aspects of writing.

What do you need to know?

Many of the writers of this book were at school at a time when explicit grammar lessons did not happen. Because they are all curious about the language which they speak, write and teach they have given themselves and are still giving themselves lessons about language. The fact that they recognise that there are linguistic niceties that they have yet to master does not mean that they are not 'good enough' users of their language. 'Negatives' and 'passives' do not give most of us many problems but you might have to give yourself lessons to check on 'pronominal reference' and 'fronted constructions'! None of us should be complacent about our knowledge level and it is very important that we all remain curious and go on learning; curiosity about language as well as teacher subject knowledge have been strands throughout this book.

We should not be fearful of teaching children in all the ways that we have been describing even while we are still in the process of developing knowledge of terminology and more difficult linguistic concepts. You need to remember that the subject of this book is teaching about the whole of writing, not just grammar. You are developing your subject knowledge on all fronts: from copying to creation, from process to genre, from composition to transcription and from monitoring and assessment to meeting the individual needs of the children you teach.

Further reading

Bean, M. and Wagstaff, P. (1991) 'The Bilingual Storyteller', in *Practical Approaches to Writing in the Primary School*. London: Longman.

Browne, A. (1993) *Helping Children to Write*. London: Paul Chapman.

Eyres, I. (1995) 'Looking for Pattern: Bilingual Readers Writing' in Bearne, E. *Greater Expectations, Children Reading Writing*, Chapter 7. London: Cassell.

QCA (1998) *Can do Better: Raising Boys' Achievement in English*. London: QCA.

Millard, E. (1997) *Differently Literate: Boys, Girls and the Schooling of Literacy*. London: Falmer.

Perera, K. (1984) *Children's Writing and Reading: Analysing Classroom Language*. Oxford: Blackwell.

Smith, B. (1995) *Through Writing to Reading: Classroom Strategies for Supporting Literacy*. London: Routledge.

References

Adams, M. J. (1990) *Beginning to Read: Thinking and Learning about Print*. Cambridge, MA: MIT Press.

Aldrich, R. (1982) *An Introduction to the History of Education*. London: Hodder and Stoughton.

Baker, C. (1996) *The Foundations of Bilingualism*. Clevedon: Multilingual Matters.

Bannatyne, A. and Cotterell, G. (1966) 'Spelling for the Dyslexic Child', in *ICAA Word Blind Bulletin* Winter.

Barrs, M. (1987) 'Learning to Write', in *Language Matters* **(2)** and **(3)**. London: CLPE.

Barrs, M. (ed.) (1990) *Shared Reading Shared Writing*. London: CLPE.

Barrs, M. (1991) *Language Matters: Thinking about Writing*. No. 1. London: CLPE.

Barrs, M. *et al.* (1988) *The Primary Language Record Handbook for Teachers*. London: CLPE.

Barrs, M. *et al.* (1990) *Patterns of Learning*. London: CLPE.

Barrs, M. and Thomas, A. (eds) (1991) *The Reading Book*. London: CLPE

Barrs, M. (1994) 'Genre Theory: What's it all About?', in Stierer, B. and Maybin, J. (eds) *Language, Literacy and Learning in Educational Practice*. Clevedon: Multilingual Matters/Open University.

Barrs, M. *et al.* (1996) 'The New Primary Language Record Writing Scale', in *Language Matters* **(3)**. London: CLPE.

Barton, D. and Hamilton, M. (1998) *Local Literacies*. London: Routledge.

Bearne, E. (1998) *Progress in Writing*. London: Routledge.

Bissex, G. (1980) *GNYS AT WRK: A Child Learns to Write and Read*. Cambridge, MA: Harvard University Press.

Britton, J. (1982) 'Outline for a Case Study', in Pradl, G. (ed.) *Prospect and Retrospect, Selected Essays for James Britton*. London: Heinemann.

Brownjohn, S. (1994) *To Rhyme or not to Rhyme, Teaching Children to Write Poetry*. London: Hodder and Stoughton.

Bryant, P. and Bradley, L. (1985) *Children's Reading Problems*. Oxford: Blackwell.

Bullock, A. *et al.* (1975) *A Language for Life*. London: HMSO.

Calkins, L. McCormick. (1983) *Lessons from a Child on the Teaching and Learning of Writing*. Exeter, New Hampshire: Heinemann.

Cashdan, A. and Grugeon, E. (eds) (1972) *Language in Education*. London: Routledge.

Chomsky, C. (1971) 'Write now, read later', in *Childhood Education* **(47)**.

Clark, M. (1976) *Young Fluent Readers*. London: Heinemann.

Clark, U. (1996) *An Introduction to Stylistics*. Cheltenham: Stanley Thornes.

Clay, M. (1975) *What Did I Write?* London: Heinemann.

Clegg, A. (ed.) (1964) *The Excitement of Writing*. London: Chatto.

Cotton, P. (1992) 'Let's All Join Up', in *Child Education* April.

Cox, B. (1991) *Cox on Cox*. Sevenoaks: Hodder and Stoughton.

Cripps, C. and Peters, M. (1996) *Collins Catchwords Teacher's Guide*. London: Collins.

Crystal, D. (1995) *The Cambridge Encyclopaedia of the English Language*. Cambridge: Cambridge University Press.

Czerniewska, P. (1992) *Learning About Writing*. Oxford: Blackwell.

Dahl, K. and Farnan, N. (1998) *Children's Writing: Perspectives from Research*. Newark, Delaware: International Reading Association.

DES (1967) *Children and their Primary Schools* (The Plowden Report). London: HMSO.

DES (1975) *A Language for Life* (The Bullock Report). London: HMSO.

DES (1978) *Primary Education in England*. London: HMSO.

DES (1982) *Education 5–9: an illustrative survey of 80 First Schools in England*. London: HMSO.

DES (1984) *English 5–16*. London: HMSO.

DES (1988) *Report of the Committee of Inquiry into the Teaching of the English Language* (The Kingman Report). London: HMSO.

DES (1989) *English for Ages 5–16* (The Cox Report). London: HMSO.

DfEE (1995) *English in the National Curriculum*. London: HMSO.

DfEE (1998a) *Teaching: High Status, High Standards* (Circular 4/98). London: DfEE.

DfEE (1998b) *The National Literacy Strategy*. London: DfEE.

Dixon, J. (1967) *Growth through English*. Oxford: Oxford University Press for NATE.

Dombey, H. and Moustafa, M. (1998) *Whole to Part Phonics: How Children Learn to Read and Spell*. London: CLPE.

Ferreiro, E. and Teberosky, A. (1979) *Literacy Before Schooling*. London: Heinemann.

Foggin, J. (1992) *Real Writing*. Sevenoaks: Hodder and Stoughton.

Ford, B. (1963) *Young Writers, Young Readers*. London: Hutchinson.

Forrestall, P. (1987) *Look it Up! A Practical Guide for Students of English*. Walton-on-Thames, Surrey: Nelson.

Fox, C. (1993) *At the Very Edge of the Forest. The Influence of Literature on Storytelling by Children*. London: Cassell.

Fulton, D. (1998) *Style and Presentation: Information for Authors*. London: David Fulton Publishers.

Gentry, R. (1982) 'An analysis of developmental spelling in GNYS AT WRK', in *The Reading Teacher* **36** (2).

Goodman, Y. (1984) 'The development of initial literacy', in Goelman, H. *et al*. (eds) *Awakening to Literacy*. London: Heinemann.

Goswami, U. and Bryant, P. (1991) *Phonological Skills and Learning to Read*. New Jersey: Lawrence Erlbaum.

Goswami, U. (1995) 'Rhyme in Children's Early Reading', in Beard, R. (ed.) *Rhyme, reading and writing*. London: Hodder and Stoughton

Graham, J. (1997) *Cracking Good Books: Teaching Literature at Key Stage Two*. Sheffield: NATE.

Graham, J. and Kelly, A. (1997) *Reading Under Control: Teaching Reading in the Primary School*. London: David Fulton Publishers.

Graham, L. (1995) *Writing Development: a Framework*. Croydon: Schools Advisory Service, London Borough of Croydon.

Graves, D. (1981) 'Renters and Owners: Donald Graves on Writing', in *English Magazine* **8**, Autumn 1981.

Graves, D. (1983) *Writing: Teachers and Children at Work*. New Hampshire: Heinemann.

Hackman, S. and Trickett, L. (1996) *Spelling 9–13*. London: Hodder and Stoughton.

Hall, N. and Robinson, A. (eds) (1996) *Learning About Punctuation*. Clevedon: Multilingual Matters.

Harding, D. (1937) 'The Role of the Onlooker', reprinted in Cashdan, (*op. cit.*)

Hardy, B. (1977) 'Narrative as a Primary Act of Mind', in Meek, M., Barton, G., Warlow, A. (eds) *The Cool Web*. London: Bodley Head.

Heath, S.B. (1983) *Ways with Words: Language, Life, and Work in Communities and Classrooms*. Cambridge: Cambridge University Press.

Hester, H. with Ellis, S. and Barrs, M. (1993) *Guide to the Primary Learning Record*. London: CLPE.

Hoey, M. (1983) *On the Surface of Discourse*. London: Unwin Hyman.

Holbrook, D. (1964) *English for the Rejected*. Cambridge: Cambridge University Press.

Holbrook, D. (1967) *Children's Writing: A Sampler for Student Teachers*. Cambridge: Cambridge University Press.

Holdaway, D. (1979) *The Foundations of Literacy*. Sydney: Ashton Scholastic.

ILEA (1985) *The Volcano: Learning through Drama*. London: ILEA.

Irving, S. (1987) 'Spelling Out Success', in *Child Education* May.

Jackson, A. and Lynch, L. (1997) *Using Multimedia to Develop Core Skills in Schools: An International Perspective*. London: Roehampton Institute for AZTEC.

Jarman, C. (1979) *The Development of Handwriting Skills*. Oxford: Blackwell.

Jarman, C. (1982) *Jarman Handwriting Scheme*. Hemel Hempstead: Simon and Schuster.

Johnson, P. (1995) *Children Making Books*. Reading: Reading and Language Information Centre, University of Reading.

Kress, G. (1982) *Learning to Write*. London: Routledge and Kegan Paul.

Kress, G. (1997) *Before Writing: Rethinking the paths to literacy*. London: Routledge.

Lane, S. and Kemp, M. (1967) *An Approach to Creative Writing*. London: Blackie.

Langdon, M. (1961) *Let the Children Write*. Harlow: Longman.

Langer, S. (1951) *Philosophy in a New Key*. 2nd edn. Cambridge, Mass.: Harvard University Press.

Laycock, L. (1996) 'Narrative and Writing: Young Children's Dictated Stories', in *Early Childhood Development and Care* (**116**).

Laycock, L. and Washtell, A. (1996) *Curriculum Bank Key Stage Two Spelling and Phonics*. Leamington Spa: Scholastic.

Lewis, M. and Wray, D. (1995) *Developing Children's Non-Fiction Writing*. Leamington Spa: Scholastic.

Marshall, S. (1963) *An Experiment in Education*. Cambridge: Cambridge University Press.

Marshall, S. (1974) *Creative Writing*. Basingstoke: Macmillan.

Martens, P. and Goodman, Y. (1996) 'Invented Punctuation', in Hall, N. and Robinson, A. (eds) (*op. cit.*)

Martin, J.R., Rothery, J., Christie, F. (1987) 'Social processes in education: a reply to Sawyer and Watson (and others)', in Reid, I. (ed.) The Place of Genre in Learning: current debates. Deakin: Deakin University.

Maybury, B. (1967) *Creative Writing for Juniors*. London: Batsford.

McKay, D. (ed.) (1970) *Breakthrough to Literacy*. Harlow: Longman.

Michael, I. (1987) *The Teaching of English*. Cambridge: Cambridge University Press.

Minns, H. (1990) *Read It To Me Now!* London: Virago.

Moffett, J. (1968) *Teaching the Universe of Discourse*. Boston: Houghton Mifflin.

Mudd, N. (1997) *The Power of Words*. Royston: UKRA.

National Writing Project (1989) *Responding to and Assessing Writing*. Surrey: Nelson.

OFSTED (1993) *The Implementation of the Curricular Requirements of the Education Reform Act: English Key Stages 1, 2, 3, 4. Fourth Year, 1992–3: A Report of Her Majesty's Chief Inspector of Schools*. London: HMSO.

O'Reilly, W. and Bostock, A. (eds) (1986) *Ideas for Handwriting*. London: DCLD.

Palmer, S. (1998) 'From A–Z' in *Times Educational Supplement*, January–July.

Payton, S. (1984) 'Developing Awareness of Print' in *Educational Review* **(2)**. Birmingham: University of Birmingham.

Perera, K. (1984) *Children's Writing and Reading: Analysing Classroom Language*. Oxford: Blackwell.

Perera, K. (1989) 'Grammatical Differentiation between Speech and Writing in Children aged 8 to 12', in Carter, R. (ed.) *Knowledge about Language and the Curriculum*. London: Hodder and Stoughton.

Peters, M. (1985) *Spelling: Caught or Taught? A New Look*, 2nd edn. London: Routledge and Kegan Paul.

Pirrie, J. (1987) *On Common Ground*. London: Hodder and Stoughton.

Pratley, R. (1988) *Spelling it Out*. London: BBC Books.

QCA (1997) *Key Stage One English Tasks Teacher's Handbook*. London: QCA.

QCA (1998) *Can do Better: Raising Boys' Achievement in English*. London: QCA.

Ramsden, M. (1993) *Rescuing Spelling*. Devon: Southgate Publishers.

Read, C. (1971) 'Pre-school Children's Knowledge of English Phonology', in *Harvard Educational Review* **(41)**.

Richardson, M. (1935) *Writing and Writing Patterns*. London: University of London Press.

Richmond, J. (1990) 'What Writers Need', in *Making Changes: resources for curriculum development*. London: HMSO.

Rosen, M. (1989) *Did I Hear You Write?* London: Andre Deutsch.

Sassoon, R. (1983) *The Practical Guide to Children's Handwriting*. London: Thames and Hudson.

Sassoon, R. (1990) *Handwriting: the way to teach it*. Cheltenham: Stanley Thornes.

SCAA (1995a) *Consistency in Teacher Assessment. Exemplification of Standards in English: Key Stages 1 and 2, Reading and Writing*. London: SCAA.

SCAA (1995b) *Planning in Key Stage One and Two*. London: SCAA.

SCAA (1996a) *Desirable Outcomes for Children's Learning on Entering Compulsory Education*. London: SCAA.

SCAA (1996b) *Teaching English as an Additional Language: A Framework for Policy*. London: SCAA.

Scardamalia, M. and Bereiter, C. (1985) 'Development of Dialectical Processes in Composition', in Olson, D. (ed.) *Literacy, Language and Learning*. Cambridge: Cambridge University Press.

Shayer, D. (1972) *The Teaching of English in Schools*. London: Routledge and Kegan Paul.

Smith, F. (1982) *Writing and the Writer*. London: Heinemann.

Smith, F. (1984) 'The Creative Achievement of Literacy', in Goelman, H., Oberg, A., Smith, F. (eds) *Awakening to Literacy*. London: Heinemann.

Smith, P. and Inglis, A. (1984) *New Nelson Handwriting*. Surrey: Nelson.

Street, B. (1995) 'Cross-cultural Perspectives on Literacy', in Maybin, J. (ed.) *Language and Literacy in Social Practice*. Clevedon: Multilingual Matters/Open University.

Styles, M. (1986) *Start-Write*. Cambridge: Cambridge University Press.

Teale, W. and Sulzby, E. (1986) *Emergent Literacy: Writing and Reading*. Norwood, NJ: Ablex.

Temple, C., Nathan, R., Burris, N. (1982) *The Beginnings of Writing*. Massachusetts: Allyn and Bacon.

Torbe, M. (1995) *Teaching and Learning Spelling*, 3rd edn. East Grinstead: Ward Lock.

Tunnicliffe, S. (1984) *Poetry Experience*. London: Methuen.

Vygotsky, L. (1962) *Thought and Language*. Cambridge, Mass: MIT Press.

Vygotsky, L. (1978) *Mind in Society*. Cambridge, Mass: Harvard University Press.

Wajnryb, R. (1990) *Grammar Dictation*. Oxford: Oxford University Press.

Washtell, A. and Laycock, L. (1996) *Curriculum Bank Key Stage One Spelling and Phonics*. Leamington Spa: Scholastic.

Wells, G. (1987) *The Meaning Makers*. London: Hodder and Stoughton.

Whitehead, F. (1978) 'What's the use, indeed?', in *Use of English* **29** (2).

Wilkinson, A. *et. al.* (1980) *Assessing Language Development*. Oxford: Oxford University Press.

Wilkinson, A. (1986) *The Quality of Writing*. Milton Keynes: Open University.

Wood, D., Bruner, J., Ross, G. (1976) 'The role of tutoring in problem solving' in *The Journal of Child Psychology and Psychiatry* **17**.

CHILDREN'S BOOKS

Aesop. *Aesop's Fables.* Translated Handford, S. (1993) Harmondsworth: Puffin Books.
Ahlberg, J. and Ahlberg, A. (1986) *The Jolly Postman,* London: Heinemann.
Ahlberg, A. and Wright, J. (1980) *Mrs Plug the Plumber.* Harmondsworth: Puffin Books.
Aiken, J. (1996) *Cold Shoulder Road.* London: Red Fox Books.
Barber, A. and Bayley, N. (1990) *The Mousehole Cat.* London: Walker Books.
Bawden, N. (1973) *Carrie's War.* London: Gollancz.
Berry, J. and Brierley, L. (1994) *Celebration Song.* Harmondsworth: Puffin Books.
Browne, A. (1986) *Piggybook.* London: Julia MacRae.
Brunhoff, J. De (1934) *The Story of Babar, the Little Elephant.* London: Methuen.
Carroll, L. and Browne, A. (1988) *Alice in Wonderland.* London: Julia MacRae
Cartwright, P. and Campbell, C. (1990) *The Diary of Neil Aitkin.* Leeds: Arncliffe.
Dahl, R. (1982) *The BFG.* London: Jonathan Cape.
Fine, A. (1989) *Bill's New Frock.* London: Methuen.
Hastings, S. and Wijngaard, J. (1985) *Sir Gawain and the Loathly Lady.* London: Walker Books.
Hawkins, C. and J. (1984) *Mig the Pig.* Harmondsworth: Puffin Books.
Hutchins, P. (1970) *Rosie's Walk.* London: Bodley Head.
Magorian, M. and Ormerod, J. (1992) *Jump.* London: Walker Books.
Moore, I. (1990) *Six Dinner Sid.* Hove: Macdonald Young Books.
Morpurgo, M. (1995) *The Wreck of the Zanzibar.* London: Heinemann.
Naughton, B. (1970) 'Spit Nolan', in *The Goalkeeper's Revenge and other stories.* Harmondsworth: Penguin.
Pearce, P. (1958) *Tom's Midnight Garden.* Oxford: Oxford University Press.
Pienkowski, J. (1984) *Christmas.* Harmondsworth: Walker Books.
Rosen, M. (1989) *The Bakerloo Flea.* London: Heinemann.
Rosen, M. (1995) *Walking the Bridge of Your Nose.* London: Kingfisher.
Scieszka, J. and Smith, L. (1989) *The True Story of the Three Little Pigs.* London: Viking Kestrel.
Story Chest (1980) *The Hungry Giant. The Monsters' Party.* Surrey: Nelson.
Thomas, R. (1987) *The Runaways.* London: Hutchinson.
Westall, R. (1992) *Gulf.* London: Methuen.
White, E.B. (1952) *Charlotte's Web.* New York: Harper Collins.

ICT SOURCES

ABLAC Learning Words, South Devon House, Newton Abbot, Devon, TQ12 2BP. Tel: 01626 332233, Fax: 01626 331464, e-mail: <educ@ablac.co.uk>
Don Johnston Special Needs, 18 Clarendon Court, Calver Road, Winwick Quay, Warrington, WA2 8QP. Tel: 01925 241642, Fax: 01925 241745; Apple Link: DJSN; Home Page: <http://donjonston.com>
Dorling Kindersley, DK Family Library, 1 Horsham Gates, North Street, Horsham, W. Sussex, RH13 5PJ, Tel: 01403 833200, Fax: 01403 274476.
Europress: Freephone 0800 454 330; e-mail <jenny@europress.co.uk>
Hunt, R. (1986) *Talking Stories for Stage 2; More Talking Stories for Stage 2; Talking Stories for Stage 3; More Talking Stories for Stage 3; Wren Stages 2 and 3 Talking Stories.* Oxford: Oxford University Press in conjunction with Sherston Software Ltd, Angel House, Sherston, Malmesbury, Wilts, SN16 0LH.
Inner London Educational Computing Centre (ILECC).
Oxford University Press (1997) *Oxford Compendium.* Oxford: Oxford University Press e-mail <ep.info@oup.co.uk>
REM, Great Western House, Langport, Somerset, TA10 9YU. Tel: 01458 253636.

Indexes

Author

Subject